THE RA  **AY**

ANDY CHRISTOPHER MILLER has worked as a professor of educational psychology for two British universities and published ten books in his field including *Child and Adolescent Therapy* (1992) and *Teachers, Parents and Classroom Behaviour: A Psychosocial Approach* (2003). He has also published book chapters, magazine and journal articles on topics as diverse as relationships, travel and mountaineering. A selection of these pieces, including his prize-winning poem for the 2011 Yeovil Literary Prize, was published as *While Giants Sleep* (2015). Andy's memoir of family, truth and secrets and what it was like to grow up in seaside Britain in the years following the Second World War has also been published as *The Naples of England* (2015)

What reviewers have said about Andy Miller's writing:

'...a distinctive voice' DAISY GOODWIN, POET,
TELEVISION WRITER ('VICTORIA') AND YEOVIL
LITERARY PRIZE JUDGE

'... can shift from lovingly recalled detail to moments of powerful
experience' TONY JONES, 2016 WINNER FOR BEST RADIO
DRAMA, WRITERS GUILD OF GREAT BRITAIN

'... the writing is lovely; lyrical, subtle, original and surprising'
CHRIS THOMPSON, RADIO AND TELEVISION WRITER
('THE ARCHERS', 'HEARTBEAT', 'EMMERDALE')

'... a terrific writer' JOHN LINDLEY, FORMER POET
LAUREATE FOR CHESHIRE AND MANCHESTER
CATHEDRAL POET

'... moving, funny and compelling' MEGAN TAYLOR,
AUTHOR, 'THE LIVES OF GHOSTS'

'... vivid and touching' FRANCES THIMANN, AUTHOR,
'NOVEMBER WEDDING'

'... pulses with life and energy' ALY STONEMAN, LEFT
LION, NOTTINGHAM

' ...immensely readable'' DR PHIL STRINGER, DEPT. OF
PSYCHOLOGY, UNIVERSITY COLLEGE LONDON

'... elegantly crafted' PROF NORAH FREDERICKSON, THE
PSYCHOLOGIST

'... there is a breath of humanity in this book'
ED DRUMMOND, POET, ACTIVIST AND LEADING
BRITISH ROCK CLIMBER

'...the best writing I've read for ages' PROF TERRY GIFFORD,
DIRECTOR, INTERNATIONAL FESTIVAL OF
MOUNTAINEERING LITERATURE

THE RAGGED WEAVE OF YESTERDAY

Andy Christopher Miller

To Irwin & Gerry with love from Andy July '18

Amcott Press

Published by Amcott Press
68 The Dale
Wirksworth
Derbyshire
DE4 4EJ

Andy Christopher Miller 2017

www.andycmiller.co.uk

Diaries ... are like conversations ... even if the conversation is with oneself. Wanting to hold such a conversation is one reason for keeping a diary; another is that it slows down time.

Alan Bennett, *Writing Home*

THE RAGGED WEAVE OF YESTERDAY

I

II

III

I

1. NINE THOUSAND DAYS

This whole business started with Lynn's email in 2012. Her husband, also called Andy and one of my oldest friends, had received a diagnosis. Any expressions of love, messages of hope, they would all help she said.

Sometimes – almost always – real shock pulls me into focus. It's all that climbing; concentrate and you'll be all right, you'll survive. Panic and you certainly won't. But this was different. That heavy safety curtain didn't drop silently and instantly into place, sealing me off from the panic and smothering the fear of losing my friend. I felt sick, disoriented and desperate instead, the real thing this time.

There certainly were memories, I had almost a whole shelf of them. '1967' was the first, still not really showing its age despite the approach of its half century. Green cloth covers, the year in gold lettering at the bottom of the black spine. '1982' has always been the odd one out, a couple of inches of blue marbled cardboard peeling away from the top of its spine. My various attempts with glue have failed to tidy its demeanour, to halt the sadness of its deterioration. On either side, '1977' and '1983' look up to the challenge of the years, but '1982' is spreading, coming slowly apart, possibly as result of damp. The most recent, the last decade's worth, are still shiny, less battered and slimmer than the earlier ones.

We'd met at Easter time in 1967, Andy and I, on a trip to Snowdonia with the college climbing club. I can't now imagine where I had found a surface level enough to rest my book so that I could produce these daily pages of neat, child-like handwriting. Maybe on my lap while I perched on a rock beneath a ring of frowning mountains or under some sombre Welsh crag

> *Wed 5th Apr 1967 - Andy Handford from Goldsmiths moved into the barn tonight bringing three boxes of provisions. The army were moving out at about 7.15 this morning. 'Would you like your beans fried, sir?' 'Eh, yes please, Simpson. Simpson, have you got your waterproofs on under your denims?'*

We'd laughed about that for a long time afterwards, many years in fact. The actual wording probably shifted in the re-telling. 'What was it that sergeant said about the waterproofs?' he sometimes asked me during our occasional conversations over the next fifty years.

I hoped it would make him laugh now as I winged the email off to Colorado, five thousand miles in microseconds.

As I searched for more anecdotes from our early times together, '1968' fell open at pages where I had inserted press cuttings or leaflets

> *Tue 5th Nov 1968 - There is a strong smell of revolution in all I see around me. I found this piece of paper in the refectory:*
> A FEW SUBJECTS FOR THESES WHICH WILL NOT BE WRITTEN:
> NATURE & HER IDEOLOGIES … KNOWLEDGE IS INSEPERABLE FROM THE USES TO WHICH IT IS PUT … PUBLICITY + SEX = FASCISM … THE DUAL DEVELOPMENT OF URBANISM & THE CONCENTRATION CAMP

Sun 17th Nov 1968 - Racialism has been stirred up again by Enoch Powell yesterday in a speech. It was very depressing to see support for him from people who are intending to teach

... URBANISM IS A POLITICAL ACT ... EDUCATION: THE FINAL SOLUTION ... REFUSE TO HAVE THOUGHTS, BEGIN THINKING ... IF YOU DON'T FUCK EACH OTHER <u>THEY</u> WILL FUCK YOU ...

Sun 17th Nov 1968 - There is a danger. Western society seems to be splitting. People are losing touch with people. From the extreme Left there is the threat (only a very mild one admittedly) of revolution, from a non-political point of view there is the call for reform throughout the social structure and a questioning of the value judgements that underlie it. To combat these there is the increase in mindless, suppressive authoritarianism and the gradual withdrawal of the liberties of the individual. And now comes this hatred from the Right

Sun 15th Dec 1968 - Friday, the term ended. We were extremely fortunate, hitching up the motorway. After two minutes a guy stopped and took us all the way, except for half a mile, to Kathy's house. He was an executive for offset lithography and a true capitalist. Not greedy or selfish but a genuine belief in progress through competition. A reasonably humane man but a servant to productivity

Distractions were everywhere

> *... the whole idea of doing the same thing in the same place day after day frightens me*

> > *... Di was telling of draft dodging among her friends in the States*

13

> *… it was very odd to be so close to* [Harold] *Wilson*

The search for anecdotes from my adventures with Andy was sabotaged at the turn of almost every page

> *…frequently I turned in my sleeping bag filling my hair with straw*

> *… morning - maths, afternoon - hour or so with the log function, afterwards an hour on the trampoline*

> *… would rate my favourite authors as JD Salinger, Thomas Hardy, Jack Kerouac and GK Chesterton*

*

Lynn's later reply gave a promising report from the early surgery and let me know how well my snippets of our early climbing days had been received

> *Thur 6th April 1967 - Andy moved into my trough and, although it is not quite long enough to stretch in and we have to buckle at the knees, another person in the trough certainly helps block the draught. Anyway, a good sleep, the best this week, and a late breakfast of corn flakes (with ice cold milk on furry teeth) followed by beans, bacon and egg. Outside the barn it was snowing so we went down to Tremadoc, hoping for a change in the weather. We were lucky. The first climb we all did was Scratch – a hard V.S. I seconded Andy and was last up which gave me the task of removing all the runners. A terrific climb. Then along to Olympic Slab … The first pitch was a bit of a mountain path, but the second, the slab, very delicate … Mark was using a runner about every two feet. A really great, really great climb… Drinking in the Pen*

*Y Gwyrdd (PYG) where I washed my hair in the
gents and had my first hot water wash in a week*

Soon, Andy himself had enough energy to write
and told me how much he remembered about these
times Why, he asked, could he remember exactly the
feel of a certain piece of rock last touched forty-five
years ago, or the subtle shades and textures of the
lichen on the boulders at Lands End, when
sometimes nowadays he couldn't remember what
items he had gone to the shop for by the time he
arrived?

*Fri 7th Apr 1967 - Down at the PYG we
actually saw Joe Brown. Back at the barn I began
talking to Andy, who seems to share a great deal
of my opinions*

I continued to rake my volumes looking for further
snippets to send, surprising myself sometimes by the
way memory had shifted certain events into different
years

*Feb 7th Feb 1972 - Andy Handford phoned
tonight .... Last weekend he cut his face in a ski
accident and is going to take out the stitches
himself. Also he went to a mediaeval banquet
organised by the Education Authority and
including the Education Officer. All that was
presented was a knife to eat with. He managed
the whole meal with his hands including
blancmange, for which spoons were provided,
and used a carafe of orange juice to wash his
hands in between courses. He doesn't think he
will be looking for promotion in Edinburgh*

Locations had become transposed and companions
whisked away through the time-space continuum

*Fri 26th May 1972 - My time sense has
completely gone but I suppose we arrived here*

just after mid-day. Cornwall certainly does not
appear so idyllic with grey skies and strong cold
winds. We pitched the tent and crashed out. I
awoke to the sound of Handford's voice, he had
come all the way from Edinburgh on the train,
leaving at 11.40 last night. The journey cost £18.
He was pissed last night and had to pack his sack
in a hurry and so has forgotten many things. We
had a good laugh about dehydrated meals
thinking they were best eaten without water. A
day's diet - Alpen, coffee with powdered milk,
Vesta curry, instant whip, Knorr soup, Horlicks

I searched for further moments. Those early
volumes were brimming with adventures and
contained few if any of the compromises that a
career, a settled relationship and a family would later
require.   As a student in London during that period,
I was at the epicentre

> … ANARCHY IS WHAT YOU LIVE EACH
> DAY … ALL YOUR TEACHERS ARE
> STUPID … MASTURBATION & THE
> GENERATION OF INSTITUTIONAL
> BEHAVIOUR … EDUCATION, OR THE
> PRODUCTION OF CONSUMPTION … WE
> TAKE OUR DREAMS FOR REALITY
> BECAUSE WE BELIEVE IN THE REALITY
> OF OUR DREAMS …

The epicentre of something. And if not actually in
the eye of the storm that was the 1960s then at least
in London SE13, the next best thing. Or rather,
coming out from Charing Cross, around the seventh
or eighth best thing, distance-wise. Actually, I lived
in fairly rough areas where going out at night often
felt quite risky. A long way from Swinging London
really but still surrounded by a sense of historic

social change being played out against a perfect soundtrack.

I became easily distracted from the task in hand, losing myself in day after day of being young and alive, some of them spent with Andy but others too detailing travels, girlfriends, hitchhiking up and down motorways, visiting friends, camping, climbing and sitting up into the early hours talking, talking, talking

> *22nd Jun 1968 - (Lewisham) In the evening went to The Plough. We sat next to Dr Caldwell whom I heard give a very left-wing view-point lecture on Vietnam some months ago. We got into conversation and it was refreshing to hear an academic, although not unfortunately a typical one, talking sense. He talked with an intensity and sincerity I seldom hear among my college contemporaries and I left feeling light-hearted*

One more page or just up until the end of the month, I told myself as I browsed. Then I would get back to the task in hand, selecting snippets from my best days with Andy to be sent at regular, frequent intervals as aid parcels. No recourse to lazy electronic search mechanisms was possible. The thousands of hand-written pages had to be leafed through manually. As I lingered over certain periods or became caught up in crazed cross-referencing over years pursuing some whim or curiosity, my feelings were anything but jubilant or celebratory.

Instead, these pages had an oppressive effect, the weight of the routines and incidental details pressing down on remembered highlights. The Devil was not *in* the detail. The Devil *was* the detail

... it was a great feeling standing in the deserted bus station waiting for the 00.19

... my physics lecturers are ignorant men

... Steve confesses that he is "psychologically rather than to any extent in practice, a homosexual"

Or, perhaps, it was a deep sadness engendered by visible proof of the passing of time, of the inaccessibility now of our youth

... the Panorama (is) in need of a kitchen porter. It would be a 48-hour, 6-day week for £8-9s-0d

... apart from grandparents this is the closest I have been to somebody who has died

... Trev led the top pitch and found the exposure ... frightening which was unusual for him

The future was all ahead of us then, now it was sagging, splitting and gathering dust on my shelf

... marvellous to be walking through heather and wild grass with the snow blowing in my face

... he showed me a 13-page letter from his tutor about one child's poem

... getting these delusions of ending up as some gasbag on education somewhere

Had I wasted too many opportunities and too much of my irrecoverable time?

Mon 25th Nov 2013 – I have a three-day writing course coming up this weekend and could do with inspiration and preparation. So, I went back to my early diaries yet again and once more noticed the sadness that these generate in me, an emotion born I think from the realisation of how much of my life has passed

Could I just junk the lot? Would life feel simpler, cleaner and clearer, without them? Would I be able to live in a less intense relationship with the future and the past if these stubborn reminders of the solidified present were no more?

Putting them to the fire had its attraction but also felt like a dangerous negation of my time on Earth. If I couldn't be rid of them was there some other option?

Editing!

Once the thought came to me my mood lifted. I would embark on the task of editing down these volumes into something of a more manageable size. Once this selection was digitally stored I could then, if I wished, destroy the physical manifestations scowling at me from my shelves.

*

I have recently read Alastair Campbell's diaries from the period when he acted as Director of Communications and Strategy to the then prime minister, Tony Blair. A newspaper review a few years ago stated that these published diaries had been extracted from over one million words that he had written during his period of office from 1993 to 2003. And as I read this it occurred to me that I had no idea of the comparable statistic for my own efforts.

Before commencing any summaries, it seemed important to acquire some basic facts and figures. But really, I was intensely curious to know whether I was anywhere near as prolific as Campbell, if I was in the same league as this driven, high achiever.

So, to set the record straight, some statistics (all measures imperial):

- I have thirty-one volumes commencing in 1967.
- Fourteen of these are in 'page-a-day' format. A further twelve take two days per page, my settled, regular format between 2001 and 2014.
- The years 1968 to 1975, I approached on a 'write when you feel inspired to record something' basis, as I have done again since 2014. These amounted to six volumes, of which three are incomplete.
- Two volumes of my page-a-day discipline, 1967 and 1977, also petered out before December 31st

  Thur 12th Nov 1967 - After dedication and perseverance my diary writing efforts appear to be coming to an end ... I shall try to finish out the year and hence preserve a quite detailed record of my life. [last entry for 1967]

In fact, these admonitions, pep talks and resolutions to return to a more disciplined approach recur through many of my early diaries.

In addition, I have two separate travel diaries - the Annapurna Circuit walk in 1988 and the Tour de Mont Blanc in 1989 – and a flimsy record of a climbing trip to California in 1990. I was either too exhausted or too drunk each evening during the American trip, in fact usually both, to summon up the focus and to pick up the pen. A cheap little exercise book, sad and angry in tone and completed after the end of a relationship in 2001, is a lonely little addition to my collection, saved only from the shredder by my sometimes-dubious need for completeness.

At the time of writing, there is an entry provided for 9,062 separate days.

The grand total of words written I estimate to be in the region of 1,627,300. I'm reasonably confident the exact figure lies somewhere within ten per cent either side of that. So, about three times the length of 'War and Peace'.

On my shelf, the books measure 2ft 3ins from end to end, spanning the fifty years between 1967 to 2016.

And while I'm at it, all together these books tip the bathroom scales at 26 lbs.

They have been transferred between my various flats and houses, their bulk increasing with each recorded year and leaving a fossilised trail, like that of some huge, gnarled lizard lumbering on through a shattered landscape towards extinction and an agitated, blood red sky.

2. ONE PART PRIG

Once I had begun to entertain the prospect of editing these diaries down to a more manageable size, one dilemma after another sprang to mind. Do I just extract the same number of pieces from each year? Say, three or five or whatever, to give a flavour of that year? And what does 'flavour' mean? If one year contains far more life events - either personal in terms of births, deaths, marriages, career, holidays, or world-shattering political and cultural phenomena – then shouldn't that year merit more extracts than a humdrum, keeping-one's-head-down and cracking-on sort of year?

I turned to the final page, December 31st, in several volumes but each time I seemed to be recording either New Years Eve parties or quiet nights in front of the television, in roughly equal measure. There was very little that provided a summary of the preceding three hundred and sixty-four days except for a couple of years in the mid-1980s when my marriage to my first wife was falling apart. I found these books and pages particularly difficult to read

> *Mon 31st Dec 1984 - I went out at 12 to be the first-footer and with kisses and hand-shakes all round, we closed the door on this dramatic and stressful year, not knowing where the hell 1985 will take us*
>
> *Tue 31st Dec 1985 - Stayed at home and quietly saw in the New Year. Glad to be closing the pages of this diary, having to open it each night has not been pleasant. A new volume will be a pleasure*

Perhaps organising my material as a sequence of chapters might prove more workable? There would be one on family, possibly, another on career. I would include one on politics or news items more generally, especially my observations and reflections on events as they had unfolded. Hobbies, especially climbing and walking, would have their own, fairly major section but so too would friends and probably, especially more latterly, the books I had read. How would I begin to tackle the ups and downs of my love life? Should I, in fact, even attempt to do so?

As I mused on various formats, the sheer presence of this total amount of words again began to weigh on me. If I wasn't careful my various editing schemes would result in a rearranged body of prose almost as long as the original.

But there were more pressing issues, literally. Well, metaphorically as well. The two challenges I first needed to address, before the sense of oppression would lift and I could attempt any method of précis, were the authorial voice of my adolescent self and the discomfort and embarrassment it generated, and my shifting and sometimes vague purposes for initiating and then sustaining the whole enterprise for so long.

*

'My Teenage Diary' was a series of half hour programmes that began in 2009 on BBC Radio 4. It was advertised as a show which involved 'celebrities opening up their intimate teenage diaries and reading them out in public for the very first time'. In each programme a guest, almost always from that staple genre of the BBC, the 'world of light entertainment', entertained a studio audience with memories and revelations from their teenage years.

So, one week we were 'inside the pubescent mind of Victoria Coren', for another Arabella Weir revisited 'her days of drinking and calorie counting'. Content of a more interesting nature was occasionally promised – Ken Livingstone reading from his 1966 diary about hitchhiking across the Sahara – but the show's unrelenting tone was quickly re-established with promises that Ken would also tell of adopting an incontinent ostrich and eating a venomous snake. Ensuring that every clichéd impression of teenage life was extracted and emphasised repeatedly, a probing host interjected regularly with quips and observations.

Why do we find the adolescent voice so excruciating and the concerns and preoccupations of teenagers so open for mockery? Does our discomfort spring from the same or a similar impulse that allows any third-rate comedian to be guaranteed a laugh or two from a mention of 'Zimmer frames'? It can only be fear that allows otherwise compassionate people to find amusement in the way that growing painfully immobile with age or infirmity can cloud out the imagined life of a child who skipped, a lover who danced and a young parent who paced a child's bedroom floor through the small hours.

Alright, I concede that such an argument may appear unduly ponderous with the parallel swollen out of shape. Even after fifty years, though, I can barely acknowledge ownership of such lines as

> *Fri 20th Jan 1967 - Got really joyful in the*
> *evening. Felt proud to be a member of the human*

*race, all those people laughing and joking in the
pub*
*Wed 8th Jan 1969 - I feel very cynical about a lot
of the people I know well at college – fine ideals
but these feel put on for the environment. I sense
middle class drives lying just below the surface*

These early years aren't all like this but, oh dear,
there is an awful lot of it. Not just in the use of terms
like 'pissed', 'human race' or 'middle class' but also
in the terrible self-righteousness that allows me to
freely accept a lift of 140 miles from London to
Sheffield from a person I then patronise as
'reasonably humane' despite being 'a true capitalist'.
And what do I have to do to be able to take seriously
the young man so easily able after barely sniffing a
bottle to convince himself of his pantheistic vision
and love for humanity?

Looking back, it would be easy to characterise
myself at this age as part prig and part prat. Better to
disown this silly young man, surely, or at least
commit his self-regarding and self-congratulatory
ramblings to the furnace?

And yet …

And yet Andy's emails confirmed that Lynn's love
and the messages from his family and friends had
helped stiffen his will to survive and recover through
the early months of 2013. Never a frequent letter
writer, he communicated with me during this period
more regularly than I have ever known.

Especially striking and moving was his comment
(which I reproduce here with his permission)

> ' … I am not content to just fizzle out, no matter
> what happens and … I'm determined to create
> some new glory days. I don't know what they will
> look like but they will stretch whatever my

*abilities are, and will take me to new and
unknown destinations. I have 8 weeks of Chemo
and Radiation to get rid of as much of the cancer
as possible, and then I figure that it's time for
some new adventures of the body and mind. I'll
keep you posted...'*

Forty-six years after their inception, these diaries
had justified their existence. Even if they served no
other function, the revitalising force of these brief
accounts had played some part in my friend's
recovery, had helped him reignite the life force. It
mattered not at all that the vehicle for these
memories was a bulk of verbiage, sometimes ill-
formed and often self-conscious, spilled across
thousands of pages.

One part prig, one part prat maybe, but also a large
portion of youthful impatience and excitement as we
all stood together at the edge of whole worlds of new
experience.

*

I would wager that most of us will react far more
tolerantly to, and be charmed most likely, by any
written fragments preserved from our childhood
years, so long as they originate from a period that
definitely predates the adolescent domain. We can
perhaps enjoy the chutzpa of other teenagers
stranded in their hormonal hiatus and sympathise,
sometimes deeply, with their monumental struggles.
Or at least tolerate them. For a while anyway.

And on a good day.

But to be reminded of our own floundering passage
between child and adult - not some sanitised version
tidied away in our memories, but the actual, blunt
diction, our idioms and vocabulary and the sheer,

impassioned assertion of self - is a hard reunion for many to make. And why should we need to?

Much later in life (and during a period when I was not completing a regular diary) a wise psychotherapist described to me an interesting model or metaphor for 'the self'. I was seeking to understand somebody who was causing me to experience high degrees of confusion and distress and the person I had consulted outlined an approach that viewed 'the self' as being composed of multiple aspects, or component selves. These might include, for example, a happy child, an anxious teenager, a frightened child, a strict mother, a kindly father, an encouraging teacher, a nurturing mother, a censorious father and so on. Events in our lives that trigger strong emotions, the shocking or frightening or perhaps the ecstatic, have the tendency to bring to the fore certain of these selves, like characters on a darkened stage leaving the others and stepping forward into the spotlight.

Such a way of viewing the psychic structure of a person was encapsulated in the clinical diagnosis of Dissociative Identity Disorder, known more popularly as Multiple Personality Disorder. Individuals who have suffered extreme trauma, particularly as a result of abuse in childhood, are more likely, so the theory goes, to have some component selves that are not well integrated with their others, denying them a balancing and reassuring presence. Thus, in such cases, a 'terrified child' self may find itself alone and centre stage, cut off from any 'protective adult' self, even unaware of its existence when confronted by emotionally challenging circumstances.

As well as a way of viewing some of the experiences of abused and traumatised individuals, such a model also describes the psychologically healthy individual. In his or her case, a mature adult self stands centre stage, aware of and united with the others, able to acknowledge and bring them all forward at appropriate moments to be viewed by the watching world.

This clinical model has not been without its critics among mental health professionals but it did for a while generate a wider cultural interest. Perhaps the best-known manifestation is the 1957 film 'The Three Faces of Eve' and, among books, 'Sybil' by Flora Rheta Schreibber. I was once sent the latter by a friend but rather put off by the florid subtitle on the front of this Penguin edition – 'The True Story Of A Woman Possessed By Sixteen Separate Personalities'. I did, though, eventually take the book with me on a walking holiday in Madeira in the early summer of 2002

> *Tue 21st May 2002 - Finished* [Melvyn
> Bragg's] *'A Son Of War', surges of emotion
> again at all the familiar scenes … Started
> reading 'Sybil', wondering a bit about the
> parallels with X, and dined locally, flirting with
> the red-haired, non-English speaking waitress*
> *Wed 22nd May 2002 - Firstly, a pleasant walk
> along a levada, the usual fascinating vegetable
> gardens, then thinning out. Up to a col, Boca do
> Risco, overlooking the northern coast. After that
> a spectacular walk along the cliff. I reckon there
> was about 2,000 feet below the path, very sheer
> in places, and mostly steep cliff above. The path
> could be seen ahead cutting a feint line across the
> cliff side. The weather was sensational, and the*

> surf and sea. I enjoyed the frisson caused by the
> need to place each foot carefully at times. I hadn't
> expected such dramatic surroundings. Down
> eventually to Porto Da Cruz, a two hour wait for
> the bus presents no problems with a café by the
> strong sea, the sun, and the pages of 'Sybil'
> zipping by
> Fri 24th May 2002 - Today I just lazed around
> at Machico absorbed in 'Sybil' ... finished the
> book in Funchal airport, moved to tears by
> Sybil's integration into one at the end and the
> continuing good news. I think I shared her relief
> after setbacks and the long sense during her
> analysis that nothing was progressing. Had I
> been at home, my tears would have flowed, but
> in the airport concourse I had to bite them back

I was persuaded by the deep humanity and the intellectual integrity displayed by this model of multiple selves. And, although not suffering from any dissociative disorder myself, this book did make a deep impression and has stayed with me. Hence, I am happy, and I aspire even to be proud, to bring occasionally into the limelight my own twenty-year old, but still adolescent, self. Even in the face of such scribblings as

> Sat 4th Feb 1967 - We caught a bus to Piccadilly
> Circus and in the wash-and-brush up saw three
> guys sprawled over a basin with a syringe in
> their hands. Is this the hub of the world? Should
> not the centre of the world be a kindergarten?

Any editing task would very quickly involve a decision about vocabulary. Should I correct errors, substitute what I must obviously have meant for what I had actually written? And whilst I was at it, would I be able to avoid making minor changes for the sake of overall accessibility and readability? Then only a few steps beyond that, could I justify refusing to lend an occasional helping hand to that self-regarding young voice? Should I not save him from himself here and there by introducing a little more wariness into his words and cunning into his constructions?

My own 'adolescent diary' isn't a subject for radio, however excruciating I may often have found that voice. It will occupy a place here though, in company with its close relations. I have made my peace. And I will retain my verbatim accounts and let the person I was once speak for himself

> *Thur 10th Sept 2009 - (N Yorks) We talked a bit and ate and when I turned in I read a little of 'The Secret Diaries of Adrian Mole' and enjoyed it far more than I expected*

*

Finding the confidence to be able to present my adolescent self before an audience does not of course, in itself, re-acquaint me with the original purposes for embarking on a lifetime of diary writing. What had originally set me off in 1967? And, perhaps more pertinently, what has brought me back in 1971, 1977, 1982, 1992, 2001 and 2007 after lay-offs of varying lengths? Have my purposes remained consistent down the decades or shifted with maturity? (In fact, is there any actual display of increasing maturity?) Was there ever any rationale beyond that of an addiction to a mythology of self, manufactured for an indifferent world?

The earliest attempt at justification appears about six weeks into the project

*Tue 14th Feb 1967 - Not a lot happened at
college today and I can see the old diary
becoming full of such boring remarks as so-and-
so enters his second day of constipation. This is
not the point of the diary: its purpose is to
attempt to capture time, by events and moods, so
that I can look back upon myself in some misty
year of 199- or even 2000 and feel again, or at
least remember, the life of the past and my youth*

Although my memory for this period is far from reliable, I am sure I will have experienced a thrill at attempting to imagine dates sketched vaguely into such a distant future. The foreseeable future at that time, thanks to George Orwell, was firmly, and with an air of finality, bounded by the distant year of 1984.

Within no time, I found myself revisiting my original aim

*Wed 13th Mar 1968 - I have just been reading
through diary entries for last summer and am
amazed at how much I had already forgotten. At
the time I thought it to be one of the most
uneventful summers and yet a lot of memorable,
distant, little moments came back while reading*

Many of my early ruminations reflect a persisting search for meaning and purpose in life, a quest obviously shared with many young people both then and across time and cultures. My diaries reflect these deliberations, most prominently in the early years when I copied out great chunks from books. When inclement weather prevented us from getting out onto the crags and mountains over Easter 1968, I had spent a considerable time in the University of London Mountaineering Club hut in Ogwen, Snowdonia, engaged in various acts of transcription. Substantial amounts of Aldous Huxley's introduction to an edition of the *Bhagavad Gita* rub up against mention of RD Laing's '*The Divided Self*' and quotes from Bertrand Russell's autobiography

> *Tue 2nd Apr 1968 - Another quote* [from Russell] - '*I have loved a ghost, and in loving a ghost my inmost self has itself become spectral. I have buried it deeper and deeper beneath layers of cheerfulness, affection, and joy of life. But my most profound feelings have remained always solitary and have found in human things no companionship. The sea, the stars, the night wind in waste places, mean more to me than even the human beings I love best and I am aware that human affection is to me at bottom an attempt to escape from the vain search for God'. I cannot agree at all with Russell but it is a very interesting paragraph with which to compare my own views*

And then, with no immediate threat to Russell's standing in British intellectual life, I entered my own thoughts on such matters.

*

By far the greatest influence on my sense of myself in the years before commencing my diaries had been the writing of Jack Kerouac, particularly his book 'The Dharma Bums'. This and his other works suffused with Zen Buddhism and riding on an undercurrent of Catholicism were for me, and for a while, a manifesto for living. No matter that his writings gave birth to a huge and ragged cult around much of the world, these books at the time felt like personal missives directed only to a very small number of isolated individuals ill at ease in an alien culture. The 'moment' mattered, both a direct and unimpeded contact with the 'now' and then its capture in the form of spontaneously created written prose. 'First thought, best thought' was how Kerouac's close friend, the poet Allen Ginsberg, put it

> *Mon 28th Jan 1969 – There have been mornings such as this tossed randomly and occasionally into my life ever since I was about seventeen. I've just come from Forest Hill to Lewisham on the bus and watched the people gossiping and hurrying about, helped the young mother put her pram in the luggage rack, shared the joke with the bus conductor as somebody gets on arguing about his place in the queue. Before I came out I'd read a little Kerouac and that did it*

The other writer who influenced me greatly at the time and who also drew on Eastern mysticism to surround the incidentals of life with a sense of the profound was JD Salinger. His three books that featured the Glass family, but much less so 'The Catcher in the Rye', seemed at the time to be written directly to me. Mediated by huge publishing and book selling industries, okay, but still essentially a direct, personal communication, part of a conversation really, one that could readily dispense with formalities and preliminaries. And that intensity, that expertly-crafted sense of intimacy, was too fragile to last, too ephemeral to provide any durable waymarks through life

> *Thur 12th Nov 1967 - Once my philosophy was that it was the overlooked incidentals in life which constituted one of the main parts of living. This was basically Salinger's influence. I seem to have strayed slightly from this way of thinking although I still FEEL it to have validity*

As well as his Zen-influenced drive to record the moment, Kerouac also inspired me to see my friends and myself as characters in a ramshackle saga scripted across the course of our lives

> *Fri Nov 19th 1969 - (Wells) We trotted around the superb cathedral with cloister-echoing choir. Very holy, especially as I was just reading 'Visions of Gerard'. Alan told me, I'd missed the papers, that Kerouac had died recently. After hearing this I read 'Tristessa'. There was a very holy passage near the end in which he describes himself as the middleman in many sexual relationships and how he sublimates them 'writing long sad stories from the legend of my life'*

I don't know about 'sexual sublimation' although, from a distance of many decades, I can now entertain the possibility that at least some of the energy spent in all that chronicling might preferably have been directed, had more opportunities arisen, towards adolescence's great obsession. And 'legend' is a bit strong, but forgivable.

I certainly enjoyed the patterns and connections I perceived to run through my life and those of my friends. And whereas I might once have imbued them with uniqueness and a legendary status, I became content to acknowledge that these were not exceptional events, that they were repeated in similar forms in the lives of many others

> *Wed 26th July 1970 - (Weymouth) Bumped into Martin L in the Duke ... He was staying up at Love Lane and said Paddy wouldn't mind. We went on up there past a beautiful harbour evening and found Ivan there. Sometimes I still get that*

> *old picture of my friends in a big kaleidoscope all appearing and reappearing in different places*

Often involving change and movement, these jottings grounded my life within the orbits of others in a very satisfying and sustaining fashion

> *Wed 22nd Oct 1970 - Maggie is now au-pairing in Paris and Alan is teaching down Gravesend way. Wild Bill is in Southampton with the Ordnance Survey. Handford's at Plas y Brenin. All these people still making patterns with their lives*

Much though I was entranced in my teens by writers such as Kerouac and Salinger, and however strongly they prompted my initial diary writing, they did also contain an inbuilt absurdity. The reason or reasons for persisting over five decades must have their origins elsewhere. It would tax the skills of the most accomplished writer to craft an interesting thousand words or so, should one ever have the desire to, let alone a million and a half, dedicated to routine bus trips or lists of friends' employment destinations

> *Fri 10th May 1967 - Approx 3.30pm. I'm sitting on bank at side of the junction outside Basingstoke where the road splits to Winchester and Salisbury. Write a more orderly sequence to the day's events later*

Action literature, 'first thought best thought' approaches, really can tumble with such ease into a chasm of banality. 'First read, last read' was one savage critic's review of an Allen Ginsberg collection.

*

The discipline of daily entries first dissolved in November 1967 and then on half a dozen other occasions (up until now).

Sometimes I made sonorous statements about my reasons for stopping

> *Sun 11th Oct 1969 - I don't know whether I shall*
> *still keep a diary as I seem to be unable to get the*
> *balm for an over-excited consciousness from the*
> *incidentals of everyday. I leave the door with a*
> *purpose nowadays and switch off my mind until*
> *it is done. Stimulation perhaps is lacking*
> *although this consciousness may only have been*
> *the diversion of a mind with not enough to*
> *occupy it. Age will bring everything*

In hindsight, it is blindingly obvious that behind this wordy peroration, my regular entries were being killed off by the rigours and demands of a teacher training course, my first footsteps into a world with professional responsibilities.

I did persist but with a less frequent schedule. Then, just over a year later, and after some respite, I found myself hankering again for the old treadmill of the daily page. Five years after beginning my first volume, the original stimulus seemed still alive and pricking

> *Fri 1st Jan 1971 - This new diary starts with a*
> *wave of the old enthusiasm for everyday*
> *incidentals. The introduction must have*
> *arrogant claims to produce a sense of self-*
> *discipline. It's been a good period for optimism*
> *.... There has been a tendency just lately for us*
> *to see the everyday as composed of trivia and*
> *consequently my 'write when the mood takes*
> *you' diaries have infrequent entries. I'm now*
> *back to thinking that I need the discipline of a*
> *'day-to-day' diary so that I reflect each evening*
> *and see the worth of all the things that have*
> *happened. Last year we went to the Isle of Wight*

*Pop Festival and had some amazing experiences
and yet I only wrote three or four lines about it*

I was four months into my first teaching post and regretting that I hadn't fixed some account of my fledgling footsteps as an adult professional (if that is what I had become), the gruelling demands and the excitement that were the lot of a probationary teacher at that time.

And, yes, I still wish that I had written down my reactions to that last gasp of the 1960s, the final, sprawling Hendrix masterpiece. Had I known he would be dead within three weeks of that hazy, midnight excess I would surely have jotted down my observations from the huge encampment known as Desolation Row.

But then, I have had a lifelong battle with a sense that the present will always be with us, will always stay fixed and much the same, despite the 26 lbs of evidence to the contrary that glares daily at me from my book shelf.

3. CODDLED AND PADDED

I had convinced myself that there were enough challenges and potential rewards to merit continuing with my attempts to edit or summarise my diaries. I had become comfortable enough with my adolescent voice where it occurred and was motivated to persist despite the distractions thrown up during the endless hours of leafing by hand that would be required. I also resolved to find strategies to sustain me when the weight of these scribbled versions of my past bore down on me, mocking, disorientating and oppressive

> *31st Jan 2014 - Quite a full and productive day on 'diaries project', still experimenting with it ... again, how 'heavy' all these volumes feel and how flat and sad I feel as I travel back and forth looking for some item I'm sure is in there somewhere'*

The central dilemma of how to chunk up this record of my adult life to date remained. Lingering unaddressed also were huge ethical dilemmas – the possibility of revealing confidences, of painting others and myself in an unattractive light, of railing, on occasion, against the wisdom of just letting the past be the past.

I felt reasonably confident about disclosing many aspects of my own character and behaviour, aware that at times I would exercise a self-censorship while acknowledging at least to myself the reasons for doing so. But I also recognised that Freudian defence mechanisms must have been kicking in at times and blocking material that might not support a sanctioned and socially-approved version of myself. Indeed, such procedures must certainly have been at work sometimes governing the entries themselves when they were originally made, either when weary before bedtime, befuddled before breakfast or during self-imposed and serious catch-up sessions a few days later with the past already beginning to slip from my grasp.

It seemed impossible to resolve these many challenges before commencing. So impossible, in fact, that I easily managed to distract myself with other pressing writing tasks.

*

But a nagging imperative continued as I carried on making regular diary entries, accounts albeit now written in the awareness that a certain contrivance might colour what was written. Perhaps it was better to commence with caution and hope that, in the process of channelling and containing the contents of the volumes, a suitable structure would reveal itself.

The course at the East Midlands Writing School therefore, when I saw it in their brochure, seemed astonishingly well-timed and directed almost exactly at my needs

> *Fri 27th Feb 2014 - Off to Leicester on the bus and trains for a course on using diaries as a source for creative writing … hopeful that reflecting about diaries, meeting others doing the same, and some input may take my own project off in directions not yet apparent to me*
> *Sat 6th Mar 2014 - Enjoying the diary course in Leicester and the journey there and back on trains. Reading Samuel Pepys on a Kindle is a strange experience, 17th century English via a digital medium. His account is fascinating*

partly because there is little if anything else
giving such a full account of day to day life. Far
more of us diarists these days - far more
accessible information all round. I struggle to
believe that any of us will produce accounts that
have distinctive qualities for generations far into
the future

This course was run by a tutor who each week brought us extracts from different diarists. In addition to Pepys we looked at Bridget Jones as well as Derek Jarman on gardening/nature diaries and Graham Greene on recording one's dreams and others. In addition to discussing these writers' differing styles and formats, we were set homework tasks to mimic each in our own entries for the ensuing week and then to present to the group at the following meeting.

Among my own kind at last, the heavy users. We could dispense with all those trivial and tentative enquiries.

'What sort of things do you write?'

'Is it therapeutic?'

'Do you ever let anybody else read it?'

'Am I in it?'

*

Sun 9th Mar 2014 - The 8.45 train to London on
a beautiful sunny morning, beginning Karl Ove
Knausgaard's 'A Death in the Family' and
expecting great things after all the reviews

Coincidentally, this book, the first of six promised volumes united under the common title of '*My Struggle*' (*Mein Kampf*, in the original) was attracting massive attention because of its detailed and extensive descriptions of the quotidian aspects of the author's life combined with a fearless, or perhaps reckless, look at intimate aspects of his growing up and family life. It seemed inevitable that I would be provoked and prodded by this literary best seller as I 'struggled' to manage my own project. Whether this influence would be benign or destructive, or whether it might in the end prove tangential or irrelevant, was impossible to predict.

*

> *Thur 13th Mar 2014 - At Leicester station on my way to the diary course, I received a text from Tom saying that Charlotte's Dad had been taken into hospital and was in a bad way. The course continues to be good but I found myself preoccupied all day with Tom's news*

And then the very next day

> *Fri 14th Mar 2014 - On the radio this morning news that Tony Benn had died about 40 minutes earlier and then a text from Tom saying that Charlotte's Dad had died early this morning*

The texts from my youngest son brought news of a family tragedy that pushed all these other matters into a white noise periphery, while subsequent pages give details of funeral arrangements, huge sadness and the aftermath of tragedy

> *Tue 25th Mar 2014 - At Newcastle early and we found the crematorium just a mile in from the A1. Driving further in along West Road looking for somewhere to sit down and eat ... the level of poverty and the collapse of an urban infrastructure were quite devastating. In my black funeral suit, clean, ironed shirt and polished shoes, I felt like a very middle class Southerner. The only place we could find was a newly-opened Lebanese restaurant, shining and sparkling, out of kilter with all its surroundings.*

> *The waitress was smiley ... and asked if we were visiting.*
> *I said we were going to the crematorium.*
> *'How lovely,' she said.*
> *'It's for a funeral'.*
> *She continued to smile.*
> *'Somebody has died'.*
> *And her face fell and she offered commiserations.*
> *The word 'crematorium' produces instant responses in my culture and it hadn't occurred to me that it would have no resonance in others*

And it is at junctures such as these that I feel most keenly the competing pulls involved in trying to devise some coherence to the presentation of my diary accounts. At this particular point, for example, it might be most respectful and seemly to pursue the matter of deaths, either this one specifically in more depth or as a link to others that have occurred occasionally and now, unfortunately, more frequently as I grow older.

Perhaps less compelling but still relevant especially as he was a noted diarist himself, I might introduce a few asides about Tony Benn, either in relation to his place in the national politics of the era that I have lived through or some more personal anecdotes about the few times when our paths have crossed or almost done so. That might lead on to a major section on my lifelong association with politics, usually more as an observer than as an activist

> *Sun 19th Jan 1984 - After having been concerned that Tony Benn might not win the Chesterfield by-election, I went over with Jane to do some canvassing. There was a steady stream of canvassers in and out of the headquarters and Jane and I were sent to canvass just two roads. It*

*was very cold. Respondents were either very
positive or concerned about Benn being an
'extremist' … People couldn't really explain in
what ways Benn was an 'extremist'*

I remember being impressed by the canvassing strategy which was aimed at identifying those constituents who were traditional Labour voters but were wavering because they had misgivings about this particular, high profile candidate. When we heard reservations of this type being expressed we were to ask and mark down whether they would like Benn to visit and talk through their worries with them personally.

Then there was Leicester, the city itself. I had lived on the outskirts for four years in the late 1990s but had first visited when a hitch hiking journey as a student encountered a dearth of lifts on the M1 and forced my friend and me to rethink our plans

*Mon 19th Jun 1967 - We were dropped at the
Blue Boar service station at 8. Hunger, thirst,
and the cold set in as the sun began to sink. Then
Dick remembered his cheque book in his bag and
we went in and gulped down eggs, sausages and
chips. We finally got a lorry which dropped us at
the Leicester slip road at midnight. The walk to
Dick's hall took almost 3 hours (9 miles?).
Chronic thirst and fatigue set in. Stopped by the
police twice*

*Tue 20th Jun 1967 - Nothing woke me this
morning but I finally got up at about 12. We
went in to have a look around but I was not very
impressed by the place* [the university]. *It was
almost exactly the place I had expected to find
after Kingsley Amis' descriptions in Lucky Jim.
Finally got a lift on to the motorway by about 3.*

*This took me to just beyond the service station
that was the site of yesterday's fiasco. Then I
picked up a furniture lorry almost immediately
which brought me into Walthamstow*

Then there was Knausgaard's tome.

Other possible offshoots again could almost
certainly be recalled upon further reflection.

*

Look at this quote from the opening chapter of a
book of dialogues between the Nobel-winning
novelist J.M. Coetzee and psychoanalytic
psychotherapist, Arabella Kurtz

> 'When I tell other people the story of my life
> – and more importantly when I tell myself
> the story of my life – should I try to make it
> into a well-formed artefact, passing swiftly
> over the times when nothing happened,
> heightening the drama of the times when lots
> was happening, giving the narrative a shape,
> creating anticipation and suspense; or on the
> contrary should I be neutral, objective,
> striving to tell a kind of truth that would
> meet the criteria of the courtroom: the truth,
> the whole truth, and nothing but the truth'
> (J.M. Coetzee in '*The Good Story. Exchanges on
> Truth, Fiction and Psychotherapy*'. Coetzee and
> Kurtz, 2015).

Well, diaries certainly do not present a well-formed
artefact. They do not pass swiftly over the dull and
boring, in fact they serve as a reminder of the extent
to which one's life comprises days, perhaps weeks
and months or even years, in which 'nothing
happened'. Nothing, that is, that would serve as an
easy shoo in for a creator of narratives.

But, and this was a new and startling revelation to me as I began to stitch quotes into the account I am now writing, diaries do achieve a purpose that both novels and personal reminiscence find hard to match. And that is the continual reminder that our lives are lived within a vast web of contemporaneous context.

We do not make sense of our lives *moment by moment* as if we are the major character in our own unique narrative. Instead, tangents, side shoots, memories, the struggle for focus and singularity of purpose and more, fill our days and are put out of reach only by the passing of time. Psychology textbooks about memory often begin with some comment to the effect that, to understand how memory functions we should first consider our minds' miraculous capacity for forgetting, for filtering out the incidentals, the thousands of them, that would otherwise crush our every waking moment. When we come to recall a particular event or period in our lives then, as a narrative-driven species, we order our account and our very memories, to ourselves as much as to others, in a way that maintains some flow and progression and omits all the other extraneous and distracting material.

Diaries provide the unsettling reminder that we do not steer through life as proponent and recipient of our own grand, or minor, narratives. And the frequency with which so many commentators return to the great power of Proust's memory-triggering madeleine cakes suggests that at some level we understand and value deeply the enormous power of the incidental in our lives.

*

So saying, back to Leicester 2014 – chilly, sunny, slipping through side streets in a city still waking up. A retired person back among the commuters, with them but not of them, energised by their bustle. New people, the network of corridors and stairways, the comical procedures and regulations of institutions, the undeniable worthiness of courses such as 'English for Beginners'

Thur 20th Mar 2014 - Enjoyed the course yet again ... we briefly discussed Tracy Emin and Andy Warhol but mainly listened to stories that everybody had written for homework. This week's task is to write our journals focussing particularly on the social side, including being really bitchy if we choose to be

Thur 10th Apr 2014 - Sorry to see the course end although I'm not sure what I really got from it. Certainly a sense that diary writing has other participants. And the company of some people who write well ... finished 'A Death in the Family' and recorded my impressions in my reading notebook:

'This book has so many rave reviews from across Europe, from countries as culturally different as Norway and Spain. Proust is the comparison that is frequently made. After reading it, all 180,000 or so words of it, I still find myself unable to form a coherent view. There is something captivating about the slowed-down account of the most mundane and everyday events - boiling a kettle, smoking a cigarette. And there is a poet at work in the Scandinavian cities and landscapes. The asides on Art are interesting and illuminative. He's good on being an adolescent and, I think, on being a son. Also, his occasional and sweeping philosophical assertions have value. Perhaps it's the daunting prospect of five more huge episodes to come that generates my caution, in case I end up committing myself to reading them all. So, I enjoyed it. The prose, the translation, is luscious and the book has certainly kept me company this past month or so. My book of the year though? Of the decade even? I'm not so sure. I think I enjoyed 'Stoner' far more'.

*

I was motivated to continue with my project. The course had revealed to me the intrinsic interest that could be found in the diaries of others and Knausgaard had shown me that it was possible to fashion what some saw as great art from the often-dismissed details of the everyday. But, whereas the first sections of this account had seemed to dictate its structure to me as I wrote, this time the starting point and the lines of development eluded me and I was easily lured back towards my half completed novel and other tasks.

Then the call for contributions to Wirksworth's annual arts festival came out. I flicked about tentatively among the drop down menus on the application form pleased in some perverse way that a range of complications – title, subtitle, format, seating arrangement, credit card details, image (all submissions must include an image comprising a specified number of pixels), suitability for children, and more – would prove just too fiddly and prevent me from making a submission before the *capitalised closing date*

> *Wed 10th Sept 2014 - Last night I presented 'A Day in the Life', a talk and discussion based on my 'diary project', at the Town Hall. I have been quite immobilised by the prospect of this, unable to concentrate or apply myself to anything else for a fortnight but also frittering away all the preparation time that I had set aside for it. Then I had a sense that nobody would come, I seemed to get lots of people saying "Sorry I can't come to your thing but ...'*
>
> *However, on the night it all went brilliantly. I had an audience of 30/30+ I would guess. Terry and Jenny Smith came with daughter Joy ... I haven't seen them for twenty-five years. Also, Graham, Jane (and others) ... People joined in with some discussion as we went along and I read selections ... It was very affirming to have a diverse audience of people who don't suffer fools giving me such a thumbs up. I am now motivated to continue. Some of us retired to the Royal Oak afterwards and conversation about diaries continued*

*

Trains again but this time the big steps up onto the *Regionale* in northern Italy. The urgent gabble over the tannoy, one or two familiar words from each sentence lifted gently out, as if by scalpel, for further, calmer analysis and translation, the message meanwhile careering on unintelligibly

> *Thur 24th Mar 2016 - The strange aspect of this journey has been wheeling behind me two cases, mostly filled to my baggage weight allowance, with my diaries*

I had failed in my planned preparation for a writing retreat in the Dolomites. My intention had been to trawl through randomly selected volumes of my diaries and pick out any extract that caught my eye. I would enter the date in the first column, so that I could find it again if I wished, the quote itself in the middle, and then any incidental thoughts, reactions or possible links or themes, in the third. Transferring this material onto my laptop would give me a manageable corpus that I could then analyse, dissect and fashion in an orderly manner far removed from the world and its internet, high in the Italian mountains.

As the date for my flight drew nearer though, I became bogged down with a sense of dread and disappointment. I had failed to prepare myself adequately. Seven solitary days of uninterrupted concentration, an opportunity available to only the extremely fortunate, would be squandered. It was not as if I hadn't tried. But the first randomly-chosen volume, '1971', yielded uninspiring material. My second choice, '2011', raised some more substantial issues, in keeping with my early aspiration for the cerebral life. But my notes were a ragged rabble of ideas, feverishly scribbled mainly after waking in the middle of the night and brought on no doubt by the focused study, the search for similarities and clashes of perspective between these two years of my life, exactly forty years apart.

*

And so it was that my departure date drew close, as did the realisation that these meagre notes would provide me with very little workable data. The rest of my volumes, their lumpen mass, by their very sullen silence proclaimed my folly, my lack of a strategy let alone its painstaking execution.

Another bag! It was the only option. Check in another bag for the plane, actually double the cost of the flight and drag these stubbornly unyielding objects behind me all the way through northern Italy. Coddle them in bubble-wrap, tuck them up safely, padded around their edges with a few pairs of socks, pants and T-shirts. Try to transport the two cases smoothly, avoiding any shocks to all our systems. Handle with care.

'Anything to declare?'

Yes, so very much.

'Any banned items?'

Innocence, connivance and hope. A flagging determination.

'A wake-up call, sir?'

Yes, a wake-up call. Yes. So very long overdue.

The train clanked away from Bergamo, my cases nestled up against those of strangers in the storage space at the end of the carriage. Biscuit-coloured blocks of dwellings with washing drying in the thin morning sunlight on some of their balconies, each contained the unnumbered histories of their many inhabitants. Construction works and half completed edifices. The sleepy halts, the urgent pointlessness of spray-can graffiti on preposterously inaccessible walls and surfaces.

Changing trains at Brescia, mine *in ritardo,* the hurrying about between noticeboards, the connections that would be missed, all the while dragging my past awkwardly and resentfully behind me. The cases, almost too heavy to lift, let alone carry up and down the steps when switching platforms at

Verona. I worried about the buffeting they were taking, the knocks and sliding rearrangement of their contents. The older ones would surely suffer, could not emerge unscathed. 1982 had always been a worry, more fragile than the rest, more inclined to give up under pressure and fall apart. The slicker, younger ones had no reason to be complacent either. Dents, scuffs and tears, a weakening of the spine, it could happen to the best of them.

The guard in her pressed grey uniform stopped by my side, punch in hand, wanting to check my ticket.

'Have you validated your journey?'

She understood!

And the next seven deskbound days would provide the answer.

The train picked up speed, hurrying northwards through the glacier-scoured valley bottom. The snow on the mountain tops to either side was now settled and serene in the spectacular Spring sunlight. The months of winter storms and blizzards, with their flagrant indiscipline, were now behind me.

II

4. THE HOPES AND FEARS

I could perhaps draw out my varying engagement with political ideas and activities over the years as a first strand for consideration.

This might provide a means whereby I can develop a voice and a method for selecting extracts around other themes, especially those of a more contentious or intimate nature. For, although politics can easily arouse passions and polarised stances, my reactions to the political might at least illustrate a more discrete and self-contained topic, one less entangled with so many other aspects of my life.

Conveniently, 1967, the year of my opening volume, was also the year in which I was first eligible to vote in a British election. Not that any sign of such a landmark can be found among its pages.

In fact – and this came as a genuine and a great surprise as I began my research – references to political matters, either national party issues or larger international affairs, are at a minimal level through the nine and a half months that I completed for that year.

Only two entries over consecutive days refer to world events, albeit of a serious and enduring nature. I had been sitting a first-year undergraduate maths exam near Regents Park on a beautiful summer's morning

> *Mon 5th Jun 1967 - I came out of the exam room feeling pretty tense and my eyes hit a newspaper placard – WAR! I came as near to fainting as I ever have and felt about to vomit. Israel and Egypt have declared war and the whole city*

seems frightened. I was feeling very scared but
after I have accepted the fact and the initial shock
has worn off, my mind has settled a little.
However, the situation is still dangerous. It
could be the beginning of the Third World War.
More abseiling tonight, a drink in the Green
Man, and a listen to the Beatles' new LP in
Mark's room. They have surpassed pop music
and are now in a sphere of their own

Remaining disentangled hasn't lasted long. The essence of a diary, mine in my younger days at least, is its idiosyncratic inter-connectedness and attempts to escape this through a scrupulously enforced editorial regime destroy the very essence of such a record.

So, a series of bizarrely juxtaposed events, each with lasting consequences – conflict in the Middle East, the release of *'Sgt. Pepper's Lonely Hearts Club Band'*, my rock climbing activities, sustained here by abseiling escapades down the six storey walls of my hall of residence, and a friendship that has been sustained over fifty years - all sit tucked closely together on this one page.

My real fear, no doubt exacerbated by examination anxieties, led to a second entry which now reads as an attempt to soothe myself and the beginning of a search for a sonorous tone in which to set down my own views and predictions about the course of important world events

Tue 6th Jun 1967 - Israel appears to have scored a
considerable victory over Egypt. The latter
claims this is due to UK and USA aid. It seems
as though Egypt is trying to provoke Britain –
they have closed the Suez Canal. How much

provocation can Britain withstand? This, I
think, is the main escalation threat

A final, minimal reference addresses the other issue that, in retrospect, has come to be widely regarded as defining the political consciousness of those times, seeping like a bloody stain through its cultural mores

Fri 16th Jun 1967 - Later did some mathematics
and ended up almost rowing with Dad about the
Vietnam War

Domestic party politics received even less of my attention. A few years earlier, while still a pupil at my grammar school, I had been enthralled by the 'satire boom' that openly ridiculed the collapsing, cobwebbed edifice that was Sir Alec Douglas-Home's socially congealed and aristocratic Tory party. Whilst I do not remember being fired with optimism and enthusiasm by Harold Wilson's incoming Labour Party, I think I would have had a sense that, with his 'white hot technological revolution' speech, we at least now had a prime minister who was only a little out of touch with the 1960s rather than one suspended within the withered and crumbling hierarchies of a previous century.

Interestingly, given how much political figures from the 1980s onwards are pressed between the covers of my later volumes, still barely contained and battling to release their poison or their optimism unto this very day, the prime minister is never once mentioned in 1967. Nor, in fact does one appear for a further four years, and this is then in a gossipy, social setting – and when he is back in opposition - rather than in the context of any striking policy or legislative developments

Sat 19th Jun 1971 - (Amersham) We got all
dressed up to go to the Labour Party Supper

> *Club – guest speaker Harold Wilson. I was*
> *looking forward to it but felt that I was sure to*
> *find the small talk boring. However, we had a*
> *great time. Talked to a lot of people and didn't*
> *find it at all a strain. It was very odd to be so*
> *close to Wilson – John came back delighted that*
> *he was bigger than him. He answered a few*
> *questions but always in an economic context. We*
> *were all very impressed by the friendliness of*
> *people in the Labour Party and, although I think*
> *it is the lesser of two evils in the capitalistic*
> *system, I may join next year*

Rather than the faceless grind of democratic governance, however, the playful anarchy that brightened various corners of 1967 proved more attractive or, at least, more worthy of note

> *Thur 16th Feb 1967 - The Students Union is*
> *holding elections for a new president and there*
> *appears to be a very big 'Don't Vote' poster-*
> *sticking anarchist group – 'the provotairiat'.*
> *Their followers appear rather easily led and*
> *generally uninformed people so we made*
> *ourselves a satirical anti-anarchist poster*
> *Sat 15th Apr 1967 - Martin has been hitchhiking*
> *around the Continent for the past two and half*
> *weeks, spending some time with the Provos in*
> *Amsterdam*

Looking at my February comment now I can see that I did not have the self-assurance to make a simple statement of principle – that I believed voting was an important act – and instead had to record my opinion in an unfortunately pompous and dismissive tone. The only reference to straightforward British party politics in my 1967 diary is a rather trivial observation from the seafront of my home town, Weymouth

> *Sun 6th Aug 1967 - There was a series of speeches from members of the young Liberals beneath the Jubilee Clock this afternoon. Although I am unable to get enthusiastic about politics, I really enjoyed seeing the speakers and constructive hecklers talking about things. Expanding beliefs, or even possessing beliefs, is something I always admire in people ... There were a few depressing remarks from the forceful, intellectual, left-wing splinter group such as 'Up with Labour' and "Ow come your lot ain't never got in then?'*

Reading this again I am struck by several things – my belief in the value of debate, the fact that I had little sympathy with 'the left', or at least with the crude manifestation I saw that afternoon, and the sarcasm by which I attempted to present to myself a more mature perspective.

Then came 1968, the year when the gently simmering surface of public discourse exploded. The huge protests against the American presence in Vietnam were taking place a dozen or so miles from where I was living in London, and in major cities all around the world.

That 1968 leaflet from the college refectory again

> FREE ELECTION OF MASTERS DOES NOT ABOLISH MASTERS AND SLAVES ... THE RATIONALITY OF OUR SOCIETY IS THE LOGIC OF MERCHANDISE ... A RIOT IS THE SOCIAL EXTENSION OF THE ORGASM ... INTELLIGENCE IS A LOCALE IN THE METHODOLOGY OF COGNITION, DO YOU HAVE ONE? ... THE 'REALITY'

OF BOREDOM & ABSURDITY ARE THE
ONLY LESSONS OF SCHOOLS...

Marching and speeches swept aside by missiles, ideals trampled beneath the hoofs of huge white horses from the stables of mythology. Paris, burning barricades around the Sorbonne, a city within a city, self-governing anarchy, the frantic teach-ins.

TO BE AS EXTREME AS REALITY ITSELF
... THE DEGENERATION OF EVERYDAY
LIFE   INTO   ...   THE   SOCIAL
CONSTRUCTION OF REALITY ... YOU
ARE THE SOUL OF A WASTE-ECONOMY
... THE SOCIOLOGIST AS POLICEMAN,
THE TEACHER AS INFORMER

Rhetoric and defiance, the truncheons and the water canon held at bay as one tense day survived through a pulsating night to become the new, succeeding dawn of the revolution. Technicolour passions and black and white television news bulletins.

DESTRUCTION: DE-STRUCTURING   ...
THIS DAY TO DAY EMPTINESS ... YOU
ARE ABSOLUTLEY FREE TO COME & GO,
TO   CIRCULATE,   BUT   ENTIRELY
IMPRISONED BY THIS FUTILE LIBERTY
TO COME AND GO IN PATHWAYS
ALREADY ESTABLISHED ...

I remember the emergency student union meetings, the cafeteria filled with leaflets and posters, the huge student body summoned for yet another lunchtime meeting to decide some stance or agree some statement. A young man with the wildness still about him addressed us. 'I've come from Paris. I was behind the barricade only two nights ago. It's holding, the revolution has begun,' he proclaimed. I remember shivering beneath the enormous weight of flimsy coincidence that seemed to have placed me in that seat in that hall at that time.

And yet, despite the clarity of my memories of this period, in my diary there is no mention. No word about the Grosvenor Square riot in March, the film footage of Vanessa Redgrave and Tariq Ali with clear complexions and convictions, leading the march. The rumours of Mick Jagger in attendance, riffing on the disarray. All passed unrecorded. I do remember being in the common room of my hall of residence and one of my friends pointing to the television news from Paris and saying that we were watching history being made. I cannot remember my reply, if indeed I made one, and that incident too went unrecorded in my diary.

If I had to pick one incident whereby I might have sensed a creative, brave and principled rebellion turning sour, it would be a Goldsmiths Students Union debate about immigration. The conservative MP, Ronald Bell, who had led the parliamentary attack on the 1965 Race Relation Act, was booked as one of the main speakers and would clearly be in front of a highly unsympathetic audience. As we settled into our seats in the crackling sense of expectation, a student I knew slightly from one of our climbing trips came along the row saying - '… as soon as Ronald Bell starts to talk we're all going stamp our feet and clap'. Then to me, not even making eye contact, '… as soon Ronald Bell starts to …'

This girl, contemptuous of debate, had struck me only weeks before as rather dull and unimaginative and very far from being a student radical and I sat discomfited through the increasing acrimony of the discussion, wondering whether a belief in the power of argument was indeed a bourgeois cold shouldering of responsibility, a moral cowardice. It was in many ways a defining moment for me and I have remembered it frequently over the intervening years. But I wrote nothing.

Or, the incident involving the egg and the nice local lady who took the minutes at the Students Union meetings. Middle-aged, tweedy, from neighbouring Brockley or another universe, up on the platform with a beleaguered executive committee unable to quell the dissent. The subsequent indignity of the debate about her dry-cleaning bill. The final empty statement. The sticky end of absurdist politics. But again, no mention.

Instead, I was writing about camping in the rain in Snowdonia with the college climbing club and subsequently catching pneumonia at the time of the March protest. Then through *'les Événements'* in May, I occupied myself with copying chunks from books by G.K. Chesterton and J.D. Salinger and several pages from Christmas Humphries' 'Zen Buddhism'. In retrospect, I suppose I was compiling, without being aware of the concept, my own 'Commonplace Book'. In that era, the prospect that I would one day be able to access a vast proportion of the world's huge archive of knowledge from a hand-held device, that such machines would themselves be commonplace, would have seemed a laughable nonsense from the furthest reaches of science fiction.

Some world events, the tragedies, certainly compelled me to make entries

*Fri 5th Apr 1968 - In Llangollen, in a
newsagents, I found that Dr Martin Luther King
has been assassinated in America and a feeling of
anger overcame me as we walked through the
beautiful little Welsh streets. Here was the sort
of peace that that man had sought but mankind
refuses to accept it*

Whereas the assassination of Robert Kennedy,
another hammer blow to youthful optimism, passed
unmentioned only two months later.

How many 'lone nuts' does it take to change a
lightness of being?

I was still unable to locate a voice with which to
capture other monumental events although
nowadays when I listen to the BBC or Pathé News
recordings from the era, I realise that melodrama or
a plummy condescension were the only major
models available and I can perhaps (apart from that
'silently rumbled') forgive myself entries such as

*Thur 22nd Aug 1968 - Silently Soviet tanks
rumbled into Prague and occupied the city. The
new liberal regime has been forcibly deposed. It is
like some dark happenings that I always credit to
what I believe to be unenlightened ages such as
the 1930s. I have become painfully aware of my
own inability to know anything about politics or
economics for certain*

I have already mentioned Enoch Powell's 'Rivers of
Blood' speech in 1968 and meeting Dr Malcolm
Caldwell by chance in a Lewisham pub but apart
from these, the only other entry in the 1960s that took
a political perspective was my comment on events
taking place well beyond our planet

*Sun 20th Jul 1969 - (Weymouth) Tonight in the
King's Arms we followed the successful Moon*

*Landing made by the Americans. It seemed quite
appropriate as I have just finished the superb
section on Kepler in* [Arthur Koestler's] *'The
Sleepwalkers'. It must be quite an important
day, this, in the history of man, something like
Columbus discovering America and yet the
whole thing is marred by the terrible pettiness
and competitiveness of the Americans. The
achievement in itself is marvellous in the true
sense of the word but it would be* ['wrong'
crossed out and substituted with *'inadequate'*]
*not to consider the reasons why it was intended
to succeed. For such notions as national prestige
I have no respect and, because of this, the day
that I longed to see when I was a child has
proved a disillusionment*

And that cynical and deflated comment, for a
decade that has marked itself out as one in which
tumultuous and long-lasting social change took
place, completes my record of the political events
that sent me scribbling as their witness, as the person
who for some reason needed to capture his own
perspective and responses before the world careered
off who could guess where?

The conclusion of an age that defined me and my
g-g-generation.

Except for the gunning down by the Ohio National
Guard on 4th May 1970 of four students protesting at
Kent State University against the Vietnam War,
deaths taken by many people of my age around the
world as a warning. Free thinking terminated by a
uniformed and uninformed obedience.

A full stop to the 1960s.

Or, four bullet points.

Why did I make no record?

*

In 1970 my wife and I obtained teaching jobs in Amersham, Buckinghamshire, one of the most conservative constituencies in the country. Work demanded much of my energy but I managed to keep a daily diary through 1971 and 1972 and then a more occasional one between 1973 and 1975. In these can be found continuing references to international and national events alongside reflections as I attempted to decide my stance on their various implications.

> Mon 23rd Aug 1971 - On the news yesterday we learned that George Jackson had been killed in a San Quentin escape bid. Jackson, a negro who had been an articulate black militant, had a book of his letters published earlier this year which impressed a lot of liberal people. He alleged that his extensions of sentence in solitary confinement were given because of his political leanings. Today he was to have his sentence reviewed and there may have been public pressure for some leniency. His supporters say that this was a frame up but, if so, the lives of two prison guards and two other prisoners is a hell of a price to pay. Before the assassination of President Kennedy this sort of political violence was unbelievable but now it is almost commonplace
>
> Tue 28th Sep 1971 - [Commenting on an article in The Guardian by Angela Davis] Hard revolution seems to have been never aware of humanity (or are these impressions merely the result of propaganda?) and yet liberal moderation seems stifled by the forces of finance and profit which control our politics. The way is

not at all clear. I agree with all of Angela Davis'
criticisms and, had I seen the things she probably
has, I would probably condone her methods. But
I haven't come face to face with the hopelessness
caused by poverty and racism. I have seen good
in people, but the people restricted by systems.
The dilemma has been depressing me a lot lately

In contrast to these violent, age-defining matters, I also attempted occasional reading trying to gain a better-informed and more historically-grounded stance

Sun 28th Mar 1971 - Chris is reading a book
about 'The Levellers and The English
Revolution' and he told me about them
Tue 1st Jun 1971 - I started reading Chris' 'The
Making of the English Working Class' which I'd
been meaning to have a go at for ages

But my appetite for history, or perhaps it was my ability to concentrate, soon deserted me and, with regret, I acknowledged, at least to myself, that I had struggled to complete even the first chapter of E.P. Thompson's voluminous classic.

The 'underground press', required reading for the counterculture in the 1960s, was also failing to provide whatever it was that I was searching for

Sun 11th Jul 1971 - Bought a copy of Ink which
I've been trying to get hold of for a few weeks
now. It is refreshingly radical but a little anti-
everything and Marxist

New acquaintances were also bringing fresh perspectives or, perhaps, confirming existing prejudices

Sat 27th Feb 1971 - Di was telling of draft
dodging among her friends in the States. It
seems unimaginable to me that me and my

> *contemporaries could be forced to wear uniforms*
> *and carry weapons and be expected to kill*

Unimaginable because, history now tells us, dry and devious Harold Wilson fought Britain's corner and managed to keep my generation removed from America's brutal firestorm on the other side of the world. The workings of our national government still seemed too out-of-step with our exaggerated consciousness, too mundane and procedural, for the implications of their crucial bargaining stance to hit home

> *Mon 6th Sep 1971 - A guy phoned up tonight*
> *about the spare room. He had an accent and I*
> *asked if he was Australian and he said, no, he*
> *was South African … and did I object? I said no*
> *but we (three) were 'a little left'. He said that*
> *would make four of us. He's coming to see us*
> *tomorrow*

Although I made no mention of such feelings in my diary, I must have welcomed the opportunity of being able to hear first-hand from a new flatmate, John, more about the day-to-day effects of the apartheid regime and the efforts to resist and topple it. In the event, an understanding of what I had meant by 'a little left' did not turn out to be shared

> *Mon 20th Sep 1971 - Back at the flat, John tells*
> *us that he sent a copy of Playboy to his brother*
> *in Johannesburg in a travel agent's wrapper and*
> *the secret police found it and have told his*
> *parents that they are going to open all their mail*
> *for the next six months*

Nonetheless, the six months or so that we spent sharing a kitchen, cups of tea and curries, did further my education in ways I might not have predicted. Mainly, this domestic proximity helped me to see the cushioned detachment enjoyed by affluent white South Africans and the trivial issues that John and his ilk perceived as major contests for liberation. A long wank to freedom, indeed!

*

If I had not written and then retained my diaries from this period, I am sure that memory would have superimposed a different emphasis on various events. The linking narrative would most probably have highlighted certain features and minimised or excluded others. I suspect that I would have romanced my radical credentials and given them greater prominence, although I would like to think that my hesitancy and conservative instincts would have also been remembered.

For instance, without the corrective presence of my tattered volumes, I would have said, with some certainty, that the developments in N Ireland from 1969 onwards had captured my attention enough to warrant a set of reflections. I know that I did view the 'civil rights' agenda pursued by a new, young set of activists like Bernadette Devlin as our British equivalent of the struggles that had occupied student cousins in the USA from the early 1960s. The rapid escalation of violence, first in terms of the unimpeded attacks on the homes of Catholics and then the reaction against a British military presence rapidly deployed, we were told, as a peace-keeping force, presented a fast moving and shifting set of loyalties and confusions.

And yet the only mention I made during those years was a vague observation about one individual I met during a final summer job before beginning my first teaching post

Sun 26th Jul 1970 - (Swindon) I've managed to
get a job in a car factory which will bring in a
few bob. It is quite bearable compared to the
(building) sites I've worked on, in fact, I'm
enjoying it. As ever, I've found an Irishman on
the staff, Dick, with whom I've managed to get
on famously. It seems strange that Ireland is
virtually undergoing sporadic bursts of civil war
and yet all the Irish I've met have come across as
beautiful, wistful people

From my experiences up until that date, the Irish
had certainly seemed to be from a land of poets and
scholars, a people The Pogues once described as
'refugees from guilt and weeping effigies'. All the
stranger then, given my affection for them, that the
era-defining catastrophe that was Bloody Sunday,
provoked not one word from me

Sun 30th Jan 1972 - This morning there was a
thin layer of snow on the ground. I got up,
quickly throwing on pullovers and gulping down
porridge, as I'd arranged to go bird-watching
with the 'S's [the family of a pupil I had
previously taught] ... *At one time the sun was*
reflecting from the snowflakes that were falling
and the air seemed to be full of glittering
particles

Was I a political dilettante, recording whatever my
gadfly attention happened to settle on as I picked up
my biro each evening? Well, yes, in many ways I was.
Despite my original fantasies about celebrating the
'now-ness' of life and capturing it as a record for
whatever years lay ahead, and my subsequent
extension into commenting occasionally on national
and world-wide events, I was not writing a

comprehensive, albeit highly personal, political history of the times

> *Wed 16th Jun 2010 - The Saville Report into Bloody Sunday was published yesterday after 12 years and phenomenal expenditure - £195m. Not only did it vindicate those killed it also said that the British Army had fired to kill and soldiers then lied to the Widgery Report. The most remarkable thing for me though was David Cameron's speech and apology in the Commons. I found it very impressive – clear and unequivocal ... Despite myself, I found myself being very impressed by him. Looking back 38 years in my diaries, I had made no reference to Bloody Sunday*

In truth, I did not have a rationale for what I wrote back in my younger days, or at least, I certainly did not adhere to one. But I am, nonetheless and inevitably, easily able to bring to consciousness images from that awful day in Derry, and have remained hooked into the spill of its consequences. The snowflakes, however, are long gone with only my words left floating and falling and turning in the sun.

So, whereas a massacre on the streets of a city that is part of the country into which I was born, somehow eluded mention, a subsequent major atrocity, this side of the water, could not be ignored – just as its perpetrators intended

> *Sun 11th Mar 1973 - Last Thursday, when there was a referendum in N Ireland on whether a link with Britain or with Eire was desired by the people, there was a series of car bombs in London. One went off outside the Old Bailey, killing one and injuring 238, and the other*

*outside New Scotland Yard. It was staggering to
see newsreel film of an office block with every
window shattered and a road with a hole blasted
into the tarmac – all this less than 30 miles away*

As the 1970s established themselves so too did a
darker mood. The optimism and idealism of the
previous decade, in all its splendour and fine-
feathered silliness, fell away, trampled underfoot by
each new outrage and calamity. Just as my own
adolescence slipped irrecoverably behind me, so too
did the country's spirited and lusty growth. Self-
conscious, grandiose and narcissistic though it
obviously was, it was very hard at times to escape the
feeling that the country's growing pains were
echoing mine and vice versa.

I moved from

> *Fri 9th Apr 1971 - We sat talking left wing
> politics – a rarity in Amersham*

and

> *Sat 15th May 1971 - Life felt idyllic sitting under
> an apple tree with pink blossom falling, drinking
> beers and running down the nasty Conservatives*

to

> *Tue 5th Sept 1972 - First day of school went OK.
> The kids seemed quite a pleasant crowd ... At
> home Dave called round and filled me in on the
> news that in Munich five Arab guerrillas had
> killed two Israeli athletes and were holding eight
> more as hostages in return for the release of 200
> political prisoners .... Just before coming to bed
> the news arrived that the guerrillas and their
> hostages had left the Olympic village by
> helicopter for a nearby airfield, but the last report
> said there was gunfire at the airport. The whole
> thing has made us sink further into the gloom*

which has surrounded the news these last 12
months or so. Perhaps my diary hasn't done the
job for me that it might have done, that of
chronicling just a little more of the news
headlines. Going to bed tonight wondering what
tomorrow morning's news will bring. I wonder
whether there is a little bit of morbid melodrama
in me, and others, that is catered for by this type
of thing. I am not sure of the 100% authenticity
of everyone's horror

and then, having moved to South Yorkshire, where
it seemed just possible to afford a house as we
awaited the birth of our first child, my own
circumstances and those of the country seemed to
grow ever more tightly intertwined, the rose around
the briar

Sun 5th Mar 1973 - (Doncaster) The
conversation has got back time and time again to
how badly off we are going to be next year. I
estimate that my take home pay is going to be
about £23pw and the mortgage repayments will
be £11. There will be an incredibly thin margin
between the possible and the impossible. It seems
as though we will recover in 3 or 4 years' time
but how long a period of desperation does it take
to stamp home for life a bitter and cynical
attitude?
I have sensed this weekend a similar feeling of
uneasiness about our society as the one I had a
few years ago at about the time that Powell made
his first immigration speech. The government
have frozen prices and incomes and there is a
wave of strikes planned for the near future by a
number of low-paid workers. Man Alive on TV
did a fantastic programme on the discrepancies

*between the way two different families had
benefitted from our 'Welfare State'. It made the
concept of 'Two Nations' seem much more
realistic. Extreme Socialist organisations are
calling for a General Strike to bring down the
present Tory government and I feel we could be
as near one now as we have ever been since the
War. I don't think that I am merely transferring
my own anxieties onto the state when I say that
there is something very wrong with our society
at the moment and I sometimes smell a
smouldering fuse*

*Sun 9th Dec 1973 - Strange rumblings in the
country. The Arabs have cut down oil supplies to
Britain and we are now threatened with petrol
rationing. The miners are preparing for a long
struggle with the government and there seem to
be a few vague hints on the radio that we are
rapidly approaching some economic disaster on
the scale of the 1930s Depression. I find it very
hard to believe that we are ever going to get out
of the desperate financial state we are in*

I was absorbed in the daily anxieties occasioned by
trying to make ends meet with a young family,
studying in every spare moment and a new job that
had seriously shaken my complacent view that I had
some natural gift as a teacher that would never let me
down. Affairs of state and the general state of affairs
tended to pass me by. In fact, my occasional diary
entries became sketchy résumés spread across
increasingly large spans of time.

There was good news though, of course. As my life
changed gear and moved into a new period of
increasing responsibility for others, the world too

seemed to leave behind an earlier dominant and horrific preoccupation

> *Thur 25th Jan 1973 - On Tuesday it was announced that an agreement between the Americans and the N Vietnamese had been reached and that the war was over. It is strange to think that the name Vietnam will soon have the same distant sound to a younger generation that Korea has to me. It has gone on for ten years – I cannot remember it not being fought – and nothing has been achieved. It is reckoned to have been the most destructive war ever and has split opinion in the West. Eight years ago my father echoed Kennedy's sentiments exactly, that if Vietnam fell the next country would follow etc. Now even he, and I feel he's representative of a lot of British people, is sickened by it although his Daily Express was still praising Nixon's intensified bombing just before Christmas*

As we quickly moved again away from a suffocating existence on a corner plot of a characterless modern estate, had a second baby and entered an intensive period of renovating a dilapidated old house in the depths of Lincolnshire, finding the time, energy and will for diary writing became impossible. One of my last entries before an eight-year interregnum referred at last and for the first time to the serving prime minister and further emphasised the instability of government in those unsettled years

> *Sun 3rd Mar 1974 - We had the general election on Thursday as Heath wanted a mandate to continue with his present incomes policy. He employed a really stupid campaign of 'reds under the beds' and it was very reassuring to see that*

the electorate didn't swallow it. The result was a
near equal number of seats for Labour and
Conservative. The Liberals polled half as many
votes as either of the others but only won 11
seats. At the moment Heath is intending to stay
in power and try to govern with a minority –
right in the middle of this chronic industrial
situation

Whatever the resolution was to be, I would not be chronicling it but would instead devote myself to house building - learning brick laying, plumbing and electrical wiring - changing career to become a trainee educational psychologist and taking a higher degree, while watching my children draw themselves to their feet, and then those feet taking them falteringly into the world of playgroups, nurseries and schools.

5. YOU GO, YOU COMMIT YOURSELF

You are alone, battling with your whole repertoire
of agitated reflexes.

Like being lifted into the world, naked, mucus-
smeared and screaming. Connected but separate, no
possibility of retreat, no way visible through the
huge, blinding fury. Sucking in breath, the
imperative for survival still rooted there in your tiny
frame when the trembling rage finally subsides.

Or, on a smooth rock face, you are holding yourself
steady with finger ends locked behind a flake or
squeezed into a crack. Your feet seek out miniscule
ledges, a sliver of instep here or there, holding you in
place. Mind and muscle under threat from gravity's
callous certainty. A vital discipline necessary to avert
the tremor in your limbs which will otherwise
escalate rapidly into huge judderings that will
dislodge you from your stance. An over-riding
prerogative to stay in control and cool the urgency.

> *Thur 10th Sept 1992 - I stood underneath High
> Tor – for some reason it has always had mythic
> qualities for me – this cliff more than anywhere
> represented the lead shield between what I could
> do and a standard that I could never reach ...
> Derek climbed well, slowly, but in control. I
> anticipated finding it very frightening, coming
> off frequently, being unable to work out moves
> despite desperately wanting to, and ending up in
> a wretched state swinging on the rope. None of
> this happened and I felt like I was confidently
> swinging up 5b moves, aware of their difficulty
> but feeling skilled and inspired enough. We had
> to abseil from the stance because of failing light*

*but we agreed to return soon. A real barrier has
been removed tonight – it feels as though it is far
bigger than just in my climbing life*

A couple of miles from my home, in the centre of that huge barrel of a cliff, I felt as alone and insignificant as in any mountain landscape or desert vastness. I could see cars below on their smooth and silent glide through Matlock Bath, hear the odd shout from a holidaymaker carried way up into my obscurity and isolation. A tight rope disappearing above connected me to Derek and prevented my falling but I would have to make that exhausting sequence of move upon move all the way until I could eventually reach him. The walls to either side curved away into the encroaching night. Each and every hold might be improbably small and cunningly hidden. I felt supremely alone, beyond being saved by anybody else, in need of the firmest of talkings-to and reliant totally on whatever it was I might have accumulated over two or three decades of rock climbing adventures.

'You go, you commit yourself, and it's the big effort that counts,' Joe Brown, the Manchester-based climbing legend, once said. And somehow I did - and it was.

We were back to complete the route the following week straight after work. 'Black Wednesday,' the newspapers called it. 'The day the British economy went over the edge'

*Wed 16th Sept 1992 - We were soon abseiling off
a tree at the very top of High Tor in beautiful
evening sunlight. Going over the top felt pretty
scary ... Derek took a long time on the difficult
crack after the first bulge and I thought we
would either be trying to get him back to the*

stance or I would be finishing in the dark. We got there, it was getting dark at the end. Any illusions I had last week about leading this were dispelled tonight. It was very steep and I suppose I was hurrying a bit, but I stayed on it (just) and did it. Running back to the car in the dark with 'sacks on our back

*

For thirty years, my diaries recorded this lush accompaniment to my life - running down sandy tracks with the curfew night buzzing, coiling rope in a wind straight off the ocean, gulls and fulmars screeching in the turmoil. A curtain of rain in a steady progression across a valley, the mountains opposite dissolving into the mist. A chill wind picking up grit on a quarry top. The need to get moving, euphoria coursing through the body. Raucous laughter, muscles stretched and swollen. The huge, outrageous camaraderie and the silent, steely streak of satisfaction.

The last twenty years now reflect a slowing down punctuated only by a yearly, nostalgic outing

Fri 5th Jul 2015 - Met Derek at Stanage … and we did 6 routes including High Neb Buttress under a scorching sun and clear blue sky. I don't see this part of the Peak District so much these days and it looked wonderful. Waves of hills, like an unsteady sea – Win Hill, Loose Hill, Mam Tor. The climbing was exacting, steep and thin, delicate in the main but also some thuggish lay-backing and chimneying … Home with grazed knees from climbing in shorts and muscles more tested than from anything in a long while

My earliest rock climbing ventures exist only in memory. Going over the top of sea cliffs at Lulworth

Cove at sixteen or seventeen with youth club leader, Bob Shepton – the Reverend Bob Shepton. Or scaling untouched rock on the Isle of Portland. First ascents and the privilege of christening routes with our very own name for them - 'Twisting Crack', 'Awkward' and 'Crow's Nest Corner'.

I knew then that I had found something enormous in my life, some crashing accompaniment to the everyday, and the sensations of those times are real and palpable even now. The absence of a precise record is no real loss but, if only I could, I would love just a quick dip into that teenage excitement, however fuelled by hyperbole it might be, to see whether I had any inkling of the course through life being charted during those dry-mouthed exertions high above a murmuring sea.

I have to be content though with beginning in 1967 with a weekend trip to the Peak District with the Goldsmiths College Mountaineering Club. Unless I had visited in the previous term, this was my first sight of the area that was eventually to become my home for many decades

> *Sat 25th Feb 1967 - Slept marvellously and was up at about 8.30. After a good breakfast of eggs, bacon and beans, we set off for Birchens. The ridge was only about 30 feet high but the climbs were quite entertaining. There was a monument erected to Lord Nelson on the top and all the names of the climbs were in some way connected with him. One really ferocious chimney, 'Kiss Me, Hardy', I soloed. Only a V Diff, but a struggle – marvellous. Did eight climbs - soloed 2, led 3 and seconded the other 3... Went into Bakewell to a pub in the evening. Exhausted.*

Part lingering adolescence and part climbing culture, my mannered phrase *'the climbs were quite entertaining'* straight away displays a participation in the deliberate understating of difficulties, a linguistic convention that was to generate both wry amusement and unnerving dread in equal measure in the coming years. So, when a guidebook used a phrase such as *'surmount the block with some difficulty...'*, a desperate grapple with the rock, perhaps with an absence of obvious hand or footholds, could be expected. *'Step delicately ...'* almost certainly predicted only friction against improbable ripples or rugosities for one's feet. *'An airy stance ...'* (these would come later on bigger crags in more mountainous environments) would be a tiny fleck of rock serving as the only resting platform on an otherwise sheer and blank face. And so on

Sun 26th Feb 1967 - After I had made last night's entry I sat by the fire talking to Maggie. She had gone off walking by herself for about five hours in the morning. The fire was dying and absolute fatigue was making me incapable of thought. Up again at 8.30, Phil cooked us a pretty decent breakfast. A clear, sunny morning as we climbed the steep hill track from the hut to Froggatt Edge. I really love that path. The first climb of the morning I led. It was a corner climb just left of the easy starter slab. Did 5 climbs in all, leading 2 and seconding 3. Felt really alive as top man for that first climb up on a rock ledge with the wind roaring in my ears. A beautiful view of the Derwent Valley with the sun on the river ... We left the hut at 4.30... Back to college by 10 and back into hall. What a bloody comedown!

Girls were in a minority in climbing clubs and the feminist revolution was still a few years from raising up its own staggering stars. Sitting with Maggie in battered armchairs before a failing fire, talking on into incoherence with the first free spirit I had ever met, not wanting it to end but not able to sustain it, I could wish for no more. Except perhaps, for a tongue in my head. The next day showered me with compensations though, adrenalin fuelled ascents of perfect gritstone, the status satisfactions of being on the sharp end of the rope, leading climbs, and the thunderous presence of Nature.

It was almost certainly on that visit that I told myself that if I ever lived in such a place I would wake each morning with a renewed sense of gratitude. No wonder returning to a men's hall of residence in S.E. London on the Sunday night was such an anti-climax.

As I trawl back through my early volumes, focusing particularly on these escapades, 1967 springs joyously from the pages as the year in which I was introduced to a number of Britain's major rock climbing areas – the Peak District, Snowdonia and Cornwall. These visits, eye-opening and breath-catching as first sightings of spectacular places to which I would return with a hungry heart through life, were also characterised by a tumbling sociability, journeys stretched through long, thin, night-time hours and a sense of being so bloody in the present, immersed in one's own vitality and surrendering willingly and full of hope to fate's ministrations.

First, North Wales, sleeping in Williams' Barn in the Ogwen Valley

> *Sun 2 Apr 1967 - The cold hit me in the night.*
> *Frequently I turned in my sleeping bag filling*
> *my hair with straw. Rising about 9 we*
> *breakfasted well on beans and egg, porridge and*
> *coffee... Motored down through roads winding*
> *through valleys, cloud-shrouded, snow-covered*
> *peaks above, placid grey lakes below, in Meg's*
> *mini – a red streak through Nature's grey and*
> *green. Down to Tremadoc. All of us did a 4-pitch*
> *route to begin with. The height was terrifying.*
> *The view from the top - the little town of*
> *Tremadoc, the sand dunes, the dam across the*
> *lake, and beyond, the sea – quiet all knowing....*
> *We descended the slippery slope after the climb*
> *with ropes slung around trees. Into a cafe at*
> *Tremadoc – hot and smoky, filled with a few*
> *climbers and old-fashioned coffee bar rockers*
> *speaking in Welsh. Mark, Meg, Maggie and I*
> *then did a Severe – 4 pitches. The exposure was*
> *terrific. But this time I enjoyed being scared.*
> *Back to the barn at about 8.30. Fried egg*
> *sandwich and coffee*

Sleep, eat, climb, repeat. On through cold, fear and elation, conscious always of testing my confidence and competence against the idiosyncratic system for grading the difficulty of climbs. Whereas in the U.S.A a straightforward and unambiguous scale was employed - 5.5, 5.6, 5.7, 5.8 and so on towards impossibility - and in the Alps the equally pragmatic I, II, III, IV, V and VI, we British had invented a sequence of descriptors possessing an echoing oddness similar to our shipping forecast regions – Moderate, Difficult, Hard Difficult, Very Difficult,

Hard Very Difficult, Mild Severe, Severe, Hard Severe, Very Severe, Hard Very Severe, Extremely Severe (this category later subdivided further into E1, E2, E3 …). Cromarty, Forth, Dogger

> *Mon 3rd Apr 1967 - Before going to sleep last night I placed a couple of sweaters under my sleeping bag. Slept solidly until 8 – warm all the time. An early start, we set off for Cym Sylin … A two-mile walk, uphill all the way, from the car to the corrie … Attempted a V Diff – The Outside Edge. As we climbed higher we met the cloud. The wind was swirling this thick wet mist around and when we reached the top, all that was visible was the patch of ground on which we were standing. Above us, the peak merged into cloud and below was a white emptiness. At the top, Chris and I were lost. We did not know the way down and were worried about stumbling over a crag. Followed, tentatively, a scree path until we heard Mark's shouting*

Each new day the life force beating a path through the privations

> *Tues 4th Apr 1967 - Froze last night. An early start after a terrific breakfast of bacon and eggs. We climbed a different route up Little Tryfan leading through. A schoolmaster on the face with a bunch of kids, shouting and bellowing. In excellent spirit … off to the Gribin Facet. Up on the face Meg and I did a Diff route again leading through. Back down and straight up a V Diff route. After this, I led Meg up another V Diff. This climb was quite exposed and when I finally finished it I felt wonderful. It seems as though I have made a big breakthrough in my climbing*

Then, after Easter in Snowdonia what used to be
known as Whitsun on the great golden cliffs around
Lands End in Cornwall

> *Sat 27th May 1967 - Left Putney at about 4 … I*
> *became more and more heavy-headed as the*
> *journey went on, but eventually we arrived to*
> *pouring rain at Sennen Cove at about 3 in the*
> *morning. The four of us all slept in the caravan*
> *… The first thing I heard in the morning was*
> *Mark's voice. Along with his mate Tim, Andy*
> *and Meg they had arrived here at 5 o'clock*
> *yesterday morning. Stepping outside the caravan*
> *found Dave and Maggie who had arrived this*
> *morning at 5*
> *Sun 28th May 1967 - This morning. Andy and I*
> *walked down to the beach and paddled in the sea.*
> *When we had walked across the beach we looked*
> *and saw that our feet were covered with oil*
> [from the Torrey Canyon spill]. *It's still*
> *about. We all drove across to Chair Ladder and*
> *after a rather tricky descent were ready to climb.*
> *Six of us did a Diff route called Western*
> *chimneys… It was a long climb and we were on*
> *it for over three hours*
> *Mon 29th May 1967 - Seconded Andy on*
> *Pegasus – a Hard Severe. A beautiful climb,*
> *especially a gripping crack to start with, a fine*
> *sloping slab further up, and a finish on a really*
> *desperate mantelshelf. We then went down to*
> *Terriers Tooth, a Hard V Diff which I led.*
> *Another tremendous climb for its grade. A tricky*
> *beginning on small granite blocks – steep,*
> *delicate and unprotected, well-protected twin*
> *cracks, then an overhang negotiated by means of*

a classic hand jam. Enjoyable abseil from the top of the pinnacle

Time to step back, take a look down the other end of the telescope. Chunking my diary entries up like this – Politics (early years), Climbing (ditto) is getting the job done, injecting coherence and continuation. But it is also feeling less and less like the life I remember.

In my previous chapter about international affairs and party politics, for instance, I brushed only glancingly against other huge aspects of my life – family, work and finances, for starters. Better perhaps that major topics like the moon landing and the Vietnam War or even significant personal accomplishments like my part-time study of psychology or installing and then, with exposed cables in each hand and the potential for blowing out the electrics for a whole village, connecting a ring main for a newly constructed kitchen, better that all these and more are perhaps omitted entirely if they cannot be given due attention?

And the same with this seemingly more self-contained rock climbing business. As I select and connect the examples in this chapter, almost whizzing again through slumbering mountain landscapes or tasting youth's audacious contempt for all the ties of tomorrow, I am failing to grasp so many strands of the web that gave a structure to those times for me – fear, confidence, ambition, competition and friendship – and all the rest. In addition, disguised amongst all this immediacy were deeper forces, slower-acting and less visible, shaping paths and a sense of identity.

Social class was one such. Except in church on a Sunday I had never, for example, met a clergyman. A distant cousin from the same council estate as myself had once become a teacher, travelling light years away from us in doing so, and that had been the height of it. Through climbing though, I met a pillar of the establishment who sometimes scaled the lamp post outside our house when calling for me. The Rev. Bob's disregard for drab respectability whilst still retaining a respected social position, appealed greatly to me, bridging immediately the gulf between our origins

> *Weds 12 Jul 1967 - At about 5, Pete gave me a lift out to Southwell to see Bob who is down again. Besides his family he brought his mother this time. Both Bob and Kate call her 'mater' which I find amusing. It's not said in an affected way. We went off down to the climbs and did Curving Crack – an enjoyable Severe, lay backing and slightly exposed. Feeling ambitious we attempted a new route near the big cave. Bob had a very tough time doing the first pitch and I had to do a substitute for this as my reach let me down. There were a few tough moments as Bob tried the second pitch but he had to come down … The tide had come in and we both got pretty wet*

> *Mon 8th Aug 1970 - Spent Sunday afternoon up the ladder cementing the back wall and talking religion with Bob*

My unsettled grammar school career had left me without that application form mainstay, a responsible person to act as a referee. Bob, British establishment to the core, must have ended up writing me scores of character references over the next half dozen years or so.

My college climbing club too granted me experiences of very different ways of life and of people I would have been otherwise unlikely to meet. Mark was a leading light, just a year older, and from a public-school background, his father being a Unitarian minister. He had packed in Alpine ascents and a spell in an Indian monastery before becoming a trainee teacher. On one occasion, he invited me and Andy to share the petrol costs for a trip to Derbyshire where, apart from two days tackling the crags, we were also allowed to rub shoulders, before their annual dinner, with famous names from the prestigious Climbers Club of Great Britain

> *Sat 6 May 1967 - Went up to Birchens where we climbed Topsail ... a bold attack on the large overhang then three Severes right next to each other and two other minor climbs... There was a party in a friend of Mark's - Nick's - house before the dinner. A very congenial atmosphere in which we downed a few pints. When everyone went to the dinner Andy and I helped their kitchen help, Kitty, to clean up the glasses*

We had been in the home of Jack Longland, later Sir Jack and Derbyshire's Director of Education. Jack Longland of 1933 Everest fame. And I had felt comfortable. The camaraderie of the climbing world, even though Andy and I were in no way eminent enough to be granted a place at dinner, the sense of a shared world in which teamwork at times ensured real, physical survival had completely over-ridden my otherwise uneasy and truculent reactions to such stark social divisions.

So it has remained. As my place on the social ladder has very gradually changed from being a hesitant kid unsure of himself to a senior university employee and then on into retirement, I have wandered fairly freely across the huge landscape of the British classes, confident enough in almost all their isolated encampments whilst never feeling completely at home in any. And never has this all mattered less than in rock climbing. My closest companions over the years have not only themselves originated from vastly different strata, they have ended up, found their place, in equally scattered destinations.

*

Beyond camaraderie, wonderful though that was, there lay a wider and more profound sense of community, one in which my sense of identity and belonging could flourish. In the mid-1960s when I first set hands upon the rock, British climbing was sustained mainly by an oral culture. With overflowing youthful arrogance, we decried the established magazine 'Climber and Rambler' – too stuffy, too conventional and dull, dull, dull. 'Stumbler and Bumbler' we called it. Old men in tweeds, smoking pipes, advertisements styled in wartime austerity fashion, in essence people who were not very good climbers presuming to speak on behalf of a new generation of risk takers who seemed vital, turned on and tuned in.

So instead of turning to worthy manuals, and before the era of accredited training centres and a cadre of patronising climbing professionals, a young aspirant had to pursue a more determined and individualised quest for guidance – or trust to luck and chance encounters.

Serendipity had brought me my two early mentors. Then it was word of mouth contact often over an informal lattice that criss-crossed the country and brought individuals into each other's presence among mountains, moors and coastal cliffs

> *Sun 14th May 1967 - A pleasant walk, despite heavy drizzle, through Forestry Commission land to Harrisons Rocks* [near Tunbridge Wells]. *The climbs are all short but very, very strenuous. The rock was extremely greasy which made serious climbing almost impossible. The technique seems to be quick jerky movements which, I don't think, is good climbing. However, we had a very enjoyable day. Saw a chap there who I bumped into halfway up a climb at Tremadoc*

Such occasions allowed first person clarifications of guide book ambiguities or the sometimes-brash opinions of other less trustworthy individuals.

'The book says the crux is at the top of the second pitch. D'you agree with that?'

> *Thur 11th Apr 1968 - (N Wales) Kathy and I walked into Capel Curig, where I saw a guy, Steve, with whom I did a climb on Portland last summer*

'Can you get anything decent in to protect those moves beneath the overhang?'

A major rendezvous for crag-starved Londoners during my Goldsmiths years was the YHA shop just off Charing Cross Road, the central source of information being Tony Willmott, the young assistant in the climbing equipment section

> *Wed 25th Jan 1967 - In the afternoon I went up to town and into the YHA shop to get a pair of*

Masters. Chap talked me into a £5.10s pair. He
kept me talking climbing for almost an hour
Sat 13th May 1967 - Went up to town with Mark
in the morning, to the YHA centre where we
spent £100 of the club's money. The chap let me
have 3 yards of nylon webbing free ... with
which to make a harness

Tony was known to regular visitors and way beyond as 'Mouth'. If you wanted an hour of his latest explorations, his forceful opinions, his recommendations, you stayed for an hour. If you wanted more, you arranged your visit to allow for more. If you could withstand a battering for even longer, you just surrendered to a verbal tour de force. If you actually wanted to buy something, and this never felt mandatory, you made an opening request as early as was possible in the stream of consciousness. At the next gap, you might be offered a '10% club discount'. More anecdotes at breakneck speed, then a breath, then the bill rounded down. A new volley of enthusiastic story-telling, anecdotes, assertion and invective. A new purchase later added to the pile to make up for the new shortfall in the bill, maybe an additional discount or rounding down, then on again, the pile slowly growing, the stories never ending. More renegotiations than in any Khatmandu marketplace

Sat 22ndAug 1969 - Last night Terry Hubble and
I went over to Portland and did Pitted Slab and
Crack Minuit against a great sunset. Terry is a
nice guy I've met on the (deck) chairs. Talking
about climbing, he suddenly asked me whether I
knew Mark Vallance. It appears that he met and
watched Mark climbing up in Wales last year

> *and, in fact, hitched a lift from the college*
> *minibus down to the Tyn-Y-Coed*

'Is it as hard as - I dunno – Crackstone Rib?'

> *Sun 14th Mar 1971 - (Peak District) The cafe*
> *was packed and in there we saw a guy who is*
> *always at Caseg Fraith hut whenever we stay*
> *there*

My main climbing pal from the late 1960s and early 1970s, Trevor, went to work at the YHA shop after he left Goldsmiths Art School, thus pulling in these threads of information and opinion even more tightly

> *Mon 10th Apr 1972 - (Snowdonia) We started*
> *out on Shadow Arete and when Bill was on the*
> *first pitch a gentle snow began. This turned to*
> *hail and then rain so we set off home ... talking*
> *with Bill yesterday, I found that he knew Trevor*
> *quite well as he was a regular customer at YHA.*
> *This climbing world is a very small one.*

'Can you abseil off, if you have to? Is there a good tree or anything?'

> *Sun 23rd Apr 1972 – (Peak District) We motored*
> *over to Stanage and did a few routes there.*
> *Standing at the top of the crag, coiling the rope*
> *with Handford, I saw a familiarly dressed figure*
> *- blue smock, denims and red roll neck. It was*
> *Bill W, last seen 13 days ago in North Wales*

All these connections, conversations, unmediated and first hand. Almost mediaeval, before print, a long lost tradition still thriving in my lifetime.

In 1971 and aged only 23, Tony Willmott lost his footing on wet, easy ground at the top of the Avon Gorge after pioneering some of the hardest climbs in the country from a very early age. I like to think that he would have been telling imaginary companions about his latest exploits, voicing his impressions, giving his opinions, in wild and fulsome fashion as his foot slipped and he fell into the void.

*

We moved to South Yorkshire at Easter 1973 because it was one of the few regions in which we could afford to buy a house. Being a father for the first time, struggling as a teacher in a new, much tougher school environment and studying in as many spare moments as possible for a degree in psychology, left little time for climbing. Left little energy or motivation either.

I did though enquire about the implications of occasional outings on the crags for my life insurance policy.

'Do you use ropes and other specialist equipment?' the firm enquired.

'Oh yes', I replied, eager to display my responsible attitude towards safety.

'Hmm', they must have thought, 'it's serious then', and whacked up my premium.

A year or so after the births of our first sons, my friend Trevor hired a car and drove up from London. We would try to dance again on the crags, to experience once more the careful choreography of movement and ascent

> *Fri 5th Jul 1974 - Trevor and I drove up the A1 and then across through Harrogate, Skipton and Settle. We were both impressed by these three towns ...*

We would discipline ourselves and use our weekend to the full.

> *... we finally pitched our tent in Eskdale at about 11.30... The next morning we drove around to*

Wasdale – virgin territory for me – to climb on Scafell.

In that lonely valley, gouged deeply into the mountains of the north west, we would rediscover our mastery of the rock. We trudged upwards through an uninspiring mist. At the foot of the cliff we searched for features – cracks, boulders and blocks - that fitted the guide book description

... we nearly had ourselves roped up and off – on the wrong crag!

A brief parting of the cloud revealed, behind us and some way across the valley, a huge cliff bounded top and bottom by the cloud – Scafell, where we should be. Trevor threw aside the guide book in frustration and it wriggled down between the boulders. With some effort we retrieved it, aired our anger and despair, pulled back some resolve and, stumbling and bumbling, picked our way across scree and heather towards our intended destination

... Finally, we set off on 'High Man via Steep Ghyll and Slingsby's Chimney'. The route was very greasy in places and neither of us felt very confident about our boots gripping

In miserable style, we completed the climb. There was no satisfaction, no sense of accomplishment, only a continuing demoralisation in which we might too easily make some irreversible mistake in the face of the mountain's huge contempt.

To be successful, to be secure, required more concentrated effort and focus than I was able to give to climbing. It was not possible. It was time to give it up. It was time to fully accept my position and to channel my need for challenge elsewhere, to move to a crumbling, old house and throw myself into making it habitable as our family expanded.

And as this new life became even busier than the previous one, I took stock, coiled up a decade of climbing memories and fell forward into my responsibilities.

6. ALSO BY THE SAME AUTHOR

October 2012 – 'A strange book and one that
I very much enjoyed. Basically, he discusses
his reading as a bookish child, he had a
terminally ill sister … and sees books as
presenting a world into which he escaped
with a sense of guilt. The book rambles as if
unsure of, or changing on a whim, its
structure. Piaget's developmental stages get
full mention, in a way that seemed
antiquated, as does Bettelheim's
psychoanalytical theories of fairy tales etc.
It's like stumbling into a 1970 teacher training
seminar. But Spufford comes across as
painfully honest and a genuine enthusiast for
books and reading. I read less than him at
that age and didn't go off to boarding school,
but he certainly captured my own private
fantasy world fuelled by words, sentences,
characters and stories' [from my review of
The Child That Books Built' by Francis
Spufford]

Profiled on the telly by Yentob, lured onto the
island by Kirsty's silky tones, or up on a stage in the
Spartan luxury of Hay's muggy encampments, these
writers are always the same. They were apparently
voracious. A great aunt let them loose among her
musty volumes, they were singled out in their early
years at school or bedridden during a long, lonely
childhood convalescence. They were complicit with
that girl's naughty little sister, they rode for their life

over Exmoor. Worried, withering and Wuthering, they came eventually, inevitably, to Pemberley.

There was no Great Literature in my childhood. Just Blyton. Just William too. And just and proper Squadron Leader James Bigglesworth, DSO, MC, DFC – 'Biggles' to we his friends.

The earliest reference to adult reading matter in my diaries, however, comes only four pages into the very first volume, when I was aged twenty

> *Wed 4th Jan 1967 - Started reading 'Far From the Madding Crowd' last night. Fabulous phrase from it to describe first two days of this year – 'a day which had a summer face and a winter constitution'*

I still have this book, awarded to my mother in 1934 at Central Girls School, Weymouth, in recognition of her 'Attendance'. It is the only remaining artefact from her childhood and, quite probably, represents the height of her academic accolades. The quotation from Hardy that appealed to me that day was transcribed into my diary in Weymouth a year or so before my parents moved from the town, from a publication that forms a link between my mother and myself to this day, and it did capture the wonderful midwinter light that haunted all about that deserted seaside resort – and does, for me, still. But it also provides a misleading impression of my reading preferences at that age.

My childhood choices were supplied directly by Weymouth Public Library, the children's section. Moving as demurely as possible among the stacks, I absorbed information by scanning titles, opening pages, author profiles and, my favourite by far, 'Also by the same author'. I carried new facts out past the issues desk as if engaged in subterfuge, in not declaring this additional knowledge secreted about my person. The date stamp slicing into a borrowing slip somewhere behind me sounded like a weapon being made ready for use but I maintained my composure and left with only my regulation allowance visible.

*

Trawling my diaries, I have so far extracted entries about early political perspectives and climbing adventures. The latter have the power to recapture many of the experiences, to put me directly back on a difficult exposed move some hundred feet or more above the ground. Or laughing, singing, wanting to hold my friends in a tight embrace, because our audacity had paid off and we had 'topped out' without mishap. The actual language I used does reasonable service to those times and, overlooking a few excesses and ill-disciplined phrases, I can expose these to public scrutiny without the fear of too much embarrassment. The political views and observations seem a little naïve in places but, again, within the bounds of youth's inexperience.

But when I come to set down my views about the books I read at that time, this changes dramatically. Some of my sentences curl up at the edges with pretension and inauthenticity and me with them

> *Wed 9th Aug 1967 - In Smiths at lunchtime I saw a copy of Hardy's 'Jude The Obscure' and, as I had a ten-shilling note in my pocket, I just had to buy it. I have been reading it tonight and it is too good for words. Hardy must be the greatest ever English novelist*

I may have studied a poem or two of Hardy's for O-level but his novels were my own later discovery. No air of failure and academic humiliation hung about his tales of Wessex. Of course, apart from a few overly-familiar passages from Dickens, I do not remember having read any other pre-twentieth century novelists, so it would have been advisable to temper a little my seemingly authoritative commendation

> ... at the present moment I would rate my favourite authors as JD Salinger, Thomas Hardy, Jack Kerouac and GK Chesterton. Most people laugh at this combination of the four ...

I doubt that I ever listed out loud these four authors to many, if any, of my acquaintances. And I am sure that I was not roundly mocked for my preferences. What, I wonder, prompted such invention? Who was I trying to kid?

> ... I enjoy Chesterton for his excellent common sense approach to subjects in his essays and the equally excellent fantasy of some of his short stories and novels

It is true that I did have a phase of reading this now unfashionable writer, picking up his novels and non-fiction for pennies from a lovely old second hand bookshop on Weymouth harbour, lured in originally by the tingling menace in the title 'The Man Who Was Thursday'

> ... Kerouac for his appreciation of nature (including human nature) and his emotional rather than factual approach (also of course his subject matter)

I can stand by that as well although it is a little vague and grandiose. But then

*... friend Thomas for the sheer involvement that
I get with his books and Salinger, well, he's more
a best friend than a favourite author*

Studying English Literature at school had not been a happy experience for me. In fact, I had not been 'studying'. I had been 'attending' - bored, lost and daydreaming. How many times were we to deride Malvolio for his vanity, painstakingly pinpointing each step down into his comeuppance? The man was a prat. Obviously. Enough said.

How could the same object – a book – be the source for such staleness of spirit when I had soared at times through childhood on the slipstreams of stories?

My disdain, my failure to grasp the protocols of the subject let alone implement them in the examination hall, was rewarded in the only way it could be. A fail grade at O-level so far down the scale, it seemed closer to an 'X', 'Y' or 'Z' than the 'A's, 'B's, and 'C's gained by my classmates.

I retreated to be among forces, masses, velocity and acceleration, maths and physics being my chosen 'A'-level subjects. Intriguing disciplines that burrowed into the hidden mechanisms of the universe, prising them apart with only the human capacity for complex abstraction and the careful conduct of experimental methods. Books and literature would have bothered and humiliated me no more had I not met an itinerant Irish intellectual during a summer holiday job between my two sixth form years. Debates and discussions, far removed from dreary classroom routines, revitalised the power of literature. But the books I began to read from that time were drawn from a subversive syllabus,

99

provocations towards self-determination and resistance.

I was looking, enthused and ready to commit, for guides on how to live.

Jack Kerouac was an early find, his '*Lonesome Traveller*' romancing a series of voyages and skid row joints and jobs. I have still never read his famous 'On the Road', discouraged by its reputation for such out-of-control hedonism and drug taking. Even if the idea of his typing away day and night on a continuous roll of paper, extemporising like one of his jazz heroes until it was complete, was such an exciting contrast to the image of literature that my school had encouraged me to loathe. '*The Dharma Bums*', however, combining the lonesome travelling, attempted adherence to Zen, solitary fire-watching on Desolation Peak and a more manageable, circumscribed level of three-day drunken parties in San Francisco, became an early spiritual manifesto.

I was still returning to Kerouac half a dozen years later and two terms into my teacher training

> *Easter Monday 1970 - On Saturday ... caught the 5.50 train from King's Cross up to Sheffield ... whisked up through the flatlands of England in a drizzling end of day light and read Desolation Angels ... I stepped out of Sheffield Midland station into a dark, rainy night, put my sack on my back and pulled my hood over my head and walked through the dark city backstreets ...*

On the same page, I was defending the writer against the criticism made by Tim, a college acquaintance and English student

> *... Kerouac is so good. Tim H, a few weeks ago, dismissed him as a syphilitic drunkard and*

junkie which seemed to me as big a crass
generalisation as one could ever find. I am
critical sometimes of his (Kerouac's) self-
centredness and yet he seems to be such a
genuine guy, and capable of such compassion.
Whether he was in fact does not bother me, he
gives me back a sensitive, Buddhist approach to
people and a sense of adventure

A spirited, even perhaps a spiritual, defence I may
have made in reply to Tim's brutal summary but it
was almost my final comment about Jack Kerouac.
His influence reappeared in 1972, helping me to put
into words what I saw and felt – helping to actually
deepen and enliven the experience – of standing on a
Cornish beach during one of our climbing trips

Sat 27th May 1972 - The weather is still not very
good but as it was getting dark Andy and I
decided to walk down to the beach ... we were
very impressed by the clump of black rocks,
draped with seaweed, standing in the rolling
Atlantic like a group of sirens. A great light to
see Cornwall in, very reminiscent of Kerouac's
description in Big Sur. Huge waves breaking out
at sea

Whether my literary tastes broadened or a
responsible and respectable career interceded, I have
only occasionally revisited this writer since that time
and then only to browse a page or two out of
curiosity. Never again a whole volume

Thur 8th Nov 2012 - The British Library. Went
to see Kerouac's scroll and attendant displays.
What a thing – after all those years. I'm back to
Weymouth, my teens, Roger and Martin [school
friends], *Dylan, 'spontaneous bop prose'. It's*
where I started – I can't judge or evaluate it

*

As with Kerouac's best seller, so too with Salinger's famous cry of adolescent alienation. I think I realised back then that it must seem like a cultivated affectation but I really did struggle with his best known, classic novel on my first attempt whilst delighting immediately in the rest of his work

> *Mon 10th Jul 1967 - Went down to the library this evening and picked up Catcher in the Rye. Read almost half of it already and think I will enjoy it this time*

No problem with his three other books that concern themselves mainly with members of the Glass family, the precocious children of vaudeville entertainers who, in their turn, each appeared on a USA-wide radio show called 'It's A Wise Child'. My earlier extract where - dare I remind and embarrass myself further? - I referred to JD Salinger as more like a best friend, was clearly inculcated by his outrageously and absurdly intimate style, unlike anything I had ever encountered.

Here from *'Raise High the Roof Beams, Carpenters'*

> 'If there is an amateur reader still left in the world - or anybody who just reads and runs - I ask him or her, with untellable affection and gratitude, to split the dedication of this book four ways with my wife and children'

and again, later, in *'Seymour. An Introduction'* where he confides for a number of pages about the nature of his relationship with this chosen reader

> 'I'm here to advise that not only will my asides run rampant from this point on (I'm not sure, in fact, that there won't be a footnote or two) but I fully intend, from time to time,

to jump up personally on the reader's back when I see something off the beaten plot line that looks exciting or interesting and worth steering toward. Speed, here, God save my American hide, means nothing whatever to me. There are, however, readers who seriously require only the most restrained, most classical, and possibly deftest method of having their attention drawn, and I suggest – as honestly as a writer can suggest this sort of thing – that they leave now, while, I can imagine, the leaving's good and easy. I'll probably continue to point out available exits as we move along, but I'm not sure I'll pretend to put my heart into it again'.

Inside my Penguin copies of these books, I had written '1965' and '1966', so my 1968 diary shows that I was remaining buoyant some two or three years later from the lift they had given to my reading pleasure – and to my continuing quest for 'Who To Be?' and 'How To Be?'

> Tue 21st May 1968 - A quote from 'Franny and Zooey', part of a letter from Buddy to Zooey:-
> 'But I swear to you that I had a perfectly communicable vision of truth... this afternoon the very instant that child told me her boyfriends' names were Bobby and Dorothy. Seymour once said to me – in a cross town bus, of all places – that all legitimate religious study must lead to unlearning the differences, the illusory differences, between boys and girls, animals and stones, day and night, heat and cold'

Mumbo jumbo? These lines do not read to me now as if from a primer on spiritual guidance. And yet they are on a par with the chunks I was at the time also copying from books on Zen Buddhism and the like. Even if I could have recognised it in 1968, I certainly would not have been able to articulate, the appeal to me of a large family, one in which siblings spoke and wrote with fizzing eccentricity about weighty matters in a style of such affectionate urgency.

I was clearly mindful, or at least reminded, of the spikey immediacy of it all when I accompanied Les, an acquaintance from my hall of residence who I did not know very well, on a drive to Clacton in his car. His fiancée, N, had recently terminated their engagement and Clacton was her home town. We mooched around the seafront, drank coffee in dull cafes and I probably regretted surrendering my day to this aimless endeavour

> *Wed 1st May 1968 - We then set off back for London, but at a garage met N's mother, who sent us back to their house. The father was a fantastic character, a retired doctor who now worked on building, a dry wit, and a real scruff with a mania for cacti. The eldest son was a physics maniac, the youngest (11), a fascist who suddenly asked me whether I was an idealist, dualist, or a materialist. He was the closest I've ever found to Salinger's Teddy. And the little girl of eight had big, dark brown eyes, a beautiful complexion, and a very adult manner which made me think of Salinger's Esmé. They were all together a fascinating family*

Again, and as with Kerouac, a writer who I had thought would accompany me through life was left behind and never, until now, revisited. GK Chesterton, in his turn, seems to have slipped through literary history, the nation's as well as my own.

*

One outcome from this current exercise involving my diaries has been the rediscovery of books that I had read in my youth. Some seem familiar and are affectionately remembered to this day. But I was certainly not aware of where and when I first encountered them and, because I had offered no evaluative comment in some cases, I have little recall of my true opinion of each at that time

> *Mon 7th Aug 1967 - Went to the library and took out Joyce's 'Dubliners' and Nietzsche's 'Thus Spake Zarathustra'*
>
> *Thur 7th Sep 1967 - In the evening I set myself down to read Thoreau's essay 'On the Duty of Civil Disobedience'. Considering that I have owned the book 3 years it is about time I read it*
>
> *Wed 13th Mar 1968 - Began reading Cannery Row today*

In the absence of additional comment, my diaries might suggest that I probably had a similar response to each. It is left to my memory, fairly accurate in this respect I believe, to supply the missing information that I did not proceed beyond the first sentence or two of Nietzsche, more than a couple of pages of Thoreau and that Steinbeck charmed me into believing that, instead of Salinger's wildly improbable Glass family, I should seek out as my ideal life companions, my own versions of Mac and the boys in their Palace Flophouse and Doc in the humble erudition of his zoological supplies store.

The book is also one of the few from the period that I have re-read more recently

*Tue 15th Jan 2013 - Reading group tonight –
'Cannery Row'. A wide range of views, which
surprised me, including a number who were as
entranced first time around ... as I had been in
1967. Instead of comparing my view of the book
then and now, I find myself considering the 'me'
then and the 'me' now, with the book as a fixed
reference point and getting much less of a look
in. It still reads very well – he writes beautiful
sentences, evokes the natural world and the built
environment very well. My earlier idolisation of
Doc, and even Mac and the boys, was not
completely sustained. The romance of the
'irresponsible' lifestyle had dimmed, the nobility
of the dropout though still resonates for me.
Varied opinion, from loving to being irritated by
it, across the group. It provoked a good
discussion*

Some of the reading documented in the early years
of my diaries did elicit some reflection, modest in
length and insight, but challenging my belief that all
confidence in my literary judgement and expression
had been torpedoed by my school experiences

*Wed 21st Jun 1967 - Bought 'The Doors of
Perception' by Aldous Huxley and 'The
Principles of Human Knowledge' by Berkley in
the college bookshop
Thur 22nd Jun 1967 - Spent the morning reading
Berkley, Huxley being too mentally tiring. The
combination of this book and the Beatles' weird
new LP are having an effect on me ... depressing
Tue 18th Jul 1967 - Finished reading Fitzgerald's
'The Great Gatsby' - a story which left me a
little flat. Everything built up so wonderfully
and then fizzled out in an anti-climax. Also, one*

> *never got to know Gatsby at all well, this was*
> *infuriating because he was an interesting*
> *character. But it was very clever*

In fact, I even attended meetings of the college's
English Society, insulated from their wider reading,
greater knowledge and analytical capabilities by a
missionary's adherence to my alternative scribes

> *Thur 4th May 1967 - Went to a poetry reading*
> *given by Dr Caroline Richards. I found the*
> *majority of her poetry too complex for me but was*
> *very surprised and pleased when she read*
> *Ginsberg's 'A Supermarket in California' as I had*
> *only remarked a couple of hours earlier how much*
> *I liked it. The college English Society, I'm afraid,*
> *do not have a very high opinion of American Beat*
> *Poetry*

Nonetheless, I was genuinely surprised to discover
that I had summoned up the bravado to offer to this
group, by whom I felt both warmly welcomed and
slightly patronised, a presentation about a loosely-
knit group of friends back home (a talk which, thank
goodness, never materialised)

> *Mon 10th Apr 1967 - I remembered that I had*
> *promised to give a talk to the English Society on*
> *Weymouth Poetry next term. So I began*
> *working on this lecture and had it half complete*
> *by lunchtime*

It is a warming realisation all these years later that,
although I was spending my college years
calibrating, measuring and graphing in a physics
laboratory and furiously copying down from a
blackboard the ancient alphabet and symbols that
were the vocabulary of mathematical proofs, I was
also reading beyond these subjects (and probably

nowhere near enough within them!) And, on some occasions, I was offering my own reactions

> *Wed 19th Jul 1967 - I am now halfway through [Joyce's] 'A Portrait of the Artist as a Young Man' and I reckon it to be one of the most enjoyable books I've ever started to read. I shall write a full appreciation of it when I finish it*

But I didn't. Write an appreciation, that is

> *Tue 22nd Aug 1967 - Stayed in tonight trying to read Camus' 'The Fall' but I am finding it difficult going. It doesn't somehow seem quite real, probably a fault of the translation*

It probably wasn't

> *Sun 27th Apr 1969 - Have been reading 'A Short History of the World' [H.G. Wells] and the majesty and width of vision that it gives of migrant tribes and races was nice ...*

Nice?

> *... Finished 'There is a Happy Land' by Keith Waterhouse – very disturbing but brilliant*

Books continued to furnish ideas, fantasies perhaps, about the tenor of an adult life that I would value and seek to attain

> *Sun 22nd Sept 1969 - A story of Steinbeck's almost brought me to tears. Perhaps I'd like to be in the position to invite friends into my place, stick a bottle of wine on the table and say 'take one glass to appreciate the taste, two to make you relax and as many as you need to keep you from getting dry as you talk!'*

Long, long before the era of reading groups, I was marking for myself an ambition that, in essence, has come to fruition over the years. Despite the comical and pretentious nature of my 1969 entry, many subsequent conversations with friends about books and reading have yielded deep and satisfying pleasures. Sometimes, perhaps, with too literal an adherence to the alcoholic prescription!

As the responsibilities of full time employment, then additional study and finally the births of my children became my priorities, so the recording of my reading diminished and eventually, along with my diary writing for the next seven years, extinguished. Not however, before a last set of entries extolled the new luxury of travel with my wife by overnight buses rather than by hitch-hiking and accompanied still, in the true spirit of hard travelling, by the latest, classic pronouncements from the counter-culture

> *Thur 11th Feb 1971 - We were up at Victoria by 5.30pm with two hours to spare before the coach. Watching the buses roll out to all different destinations was quite an enjoyable experience. And then ours came. An embodiment of all my dreams about greyhound buses – streamlined-shaped windows, reclining seats, individual reading lights and air fans. I sat there enthralled. I read Rolling Stone, which was lengthy as usual, and then some of 'One Flew Over the Cuckoo's Nest'.*
>
> *Mon 15th Feb 1971 - We are now on the coach home at 9.45pm somewhere between Edinburgh and Newcastle, and I've just finished reading 'One Flew Over the Cuckoo's Nest', which is a brilliant modern novel and about which I must write more ... when the book will keep still*

Intoxicated by the prose, disturbed sleep, and unfamiliar towns slipping by well beyond midnight, the last of such journeys coupled, intertwined even, with an intense appreciation of a book came at the end of a marvellous fortnight that included hitch-hiking with my wife from Amersham to a six-day house party in North Devon, bus and coach trips from there to Snowdonia, adventures in the mountains and then a journey to Manchester, my first visit, squashed in the back of a mini-van driven by friends

> *Tue 11th Apr 1972 - It was bad weather again, so we decided to go to Manchester with Rich and Angie ... We got to (an) old brick Manchester suburb at teatime. These two have friends who live in the next-door flat and both living rooms have hashish plants growing on the tables under time-switched lamps.*
>
> *Wed 12th Apr 1972 - Slept really well last night with our bags put down on a four-poster bed in the flat next door. Been reading Rick's 'Electric Kool-Aid Acid Test'... Kesey and his Merry Pranksters were at full height in '64 when the reverberations of his acid tripping weren't to be felt over here until '67.*
>
> *Thur 13thApr 1972 - Kesey says 'you're either on the bus or off the bus'. Our bus kept stopping at places such as Newcastle under Lyme and Stoke on Trent. Napping and finally dropping off, waking up on the last part of the rural A1. The big journey comes to an end. A strange, long, enlightening time. All sorts of images remain – Petronella high on mescaline goofing out in the dance hall, smoky room, hothouse; those learies with ultra-violet, stiff starched, stiff collars; Penny with coat flapping on a flat rock on a headland; sun-happy, green, Herefordshire; Llandudno's fairy light crescent bay; mist on the Glydders, lost on the Glydders, Clogwyn*

> *Cneiffon through the mist, rain, half-hippie Bill,*
> *Manchester, Rick, long silences, hi-fi sets – an*
> *incredible collage continuing into Tom Wolfe*

Then I was off the bus. It was the end of my 1960s. It would be a decade, probably two, before I returned to regular reading beyond professional requirements. And I would come back with substantially altered perspectives and sensibilities.

*

Being teachers for two to three years before acquiring family responsibilities did mean that my wife and I could afford camping and climbing holidays with friends in the Alps during the summer breaks, times for extended periods of relaxed reading on rest days and during prolonged spells of staying low in the valleys during storms

> *Sun 13th Aug 1972 - (Italian Alps) Spent the*
> *afternoon lying in the cool under the trees*
> *reading Koestler. Handford is reading 'The*
> *Sleepwalkers' and as quite a bit of my book*
> *overlaps his it is good for conversation. He was*
> *mentioning some time through the day that*
> *Galileo and Plato didn't emerge as very free*
> *thinking characters …*

I had been deeply impressed by Koestler's detailed and engaging history of the great cosmologists who had attempted to measure and thus build accurate theoretical models of the planets' movements through the heavens. With enthusiasm, I had launched straight in to *'The Act of Creation'*, the second book in this magnificent loose trilogy

> *… As we were all lying in the tent Isabel noticed*
> *a great big centipede crawling up the wall. While*
> *we were all cowering Handford was jumping*
> *about in his purple underpants thumbing*

> *through 'The Sleepwalkers' shouting 'Let me get*
> *at him with Galileo, where's Galileo! What about*
> *Plato, Aristotle will do'*

The shadow from our flickering light elongated the length of insect, legs scrabbling in their multitude every which way against the tent wall, a huge head tracking from side to side. With sleeping bags pulled up to and in around our necks, we huddled together in the furthest corner, our cries of disgust and alarm forcing him to snap the book closed on the gigantic creature. He threw the volume out through the tent flap, leaping after it to tread down firmly onto the top cover.

Our nerves eventually settled and sleep eventually came. And the next morning I was the first to emerge and examine the discarded book and carcass. Insect detritus extended from both the top and bottom. I gingerly opened it at its grotesque bookmark and found several pages to either side stained through with its vulgar juices.

But our rising distress the night before had panicked Handford and it was my book that had performed the execution

> *… In the end he had picked up 'The Act of*
> *Creation' by mistake and got him with poor old,*
> *inoffensive Louis Pasteur*

*

The fourth of the proudly asserted quartet of my favourites from 1967, Thomas Hardy, would then wait another forty years again before his return to my attention

> *Wed 13th Jan 2013 - Finished 'The Return of the*
> *Native'. Thoroughly enjoyed it and*
> *reacquainting myself with Hardy. I read four of*
> *Hardy's big novels back in the late '60s and*

never quite got to this one. Then, when reading
Claire Tomalin's biography a couple of years
ago, realised I may have missed another classic. I
had. After finishing it I wanted to carry on
living in its landscape of heathland and
language. Prof John Bayley writes an excellent
introductory essay in my Everyman edition and
describes Hardy's view of people as 'mere scraps
of consciousness swirling in an indifferent
universe' (or some such). The intense presence of
Egdon Heath, like the lead character, makes this
a wonderful book about landscape (although
evoking Derbyshire far more than Dorset for
me), but also about tumultuous lives lived in an
earlier time. I loved this book – Hardy is so
modern in some ways, his characters had me
thinking of people I know and have known. And
I see the feelings of my younger self, and still
some of me now, in a number of his protagonists.
Have gone straight out and ordered The
Woodlanders.

And what about that hated English Literature 'O'-
level, my helplessness and hopelessness in the face of
what I had experienced as an effete and elitist
pursuit? Had I derived any benefits, any
unappreciated lessons through my life?

Tue 28th Jul 2009 - (Ambleside) Rain in the
night and on awakening. Decided to go to
Wordsworth's cottage… a pleasant four miles
along tracks and paths … despite all the rain.
Dove Cottage was magical, dark with coal fires
in the downstairs rooms. Cramped living space
for a household of increasing size … Tennyson
apparently said you get three hot meals a day at
the Wordsworth's and two of them are porridge.

Upstairs the guide lady showed us the room where Wordsworth wrote a lot of his best-known poetry, including 'Upon Westminster Bridge'. I had a lump in my throat.

We were a ragged little group of strangers, dripping onto floors, steaming in front of the fires. I looked at the poet's chaise longue and out through the open window. Grasmere dissolved. Instead, through the drizzle, miles of featureless water swept in to Weymouth Bay.

Did Wordsworth pace this floor, casting around for the words to anchor his mood, unable to sit comfortably for long upon such an austere piece of furniture? I had walked our living room struggling to fix them, chanting silently to myself, accelerating with the fear of having to recite in class the next day. Had he reviewed, revised, reconsidered, looked beyond the view from this window into his heart?

Earth has not anything to show more fair.

I had stared straight ahead from the back of the class, been interrupted one line in and ordered to speak up and to start again. As his verses formed, when the effort melted away and the force of feeling drove the lines, had his life, his wanderings, this valley and this room all fused into the intensity of the present? This poem has accompanied me through half a century and more. It was taught me in buildings now demolished by people now long dead.

Dull would he be of soul.

How light the gifts we carry the longest.

How slight the triggers to such profound coincidences of time and place, words and passion.

Who indeed could pass by?

7. SCRAPS OF NAVIGATION

22nd Aug 1969 - My degree results arrived last week, proving ... disappointing. I don't know whether to re-sit the examination next summer or not yet. I feel inclined at the moment to forget the whole silly business. It produces a sickening feeling to think that you receive absolutely nothing for three years' reasonably hard work

I had failed my degree.

Somebody from an older generation, my Dad for example, might have queried what I actually knew about or meant by 'reasonably hard work'. And they would be right to ask. I had few models of studious behaviour to whom I could turn. There were none really. What did academic endeavour really look like? How did it feel? Such notions had dogged me all through my education up until that time.

*

I am a 'beneficiary' of the grammar school system. An ungrateful beneficiary.

Aptitude, potential, intelligence – educators were obsessed by such notions. And I seemed to have enough in restless residency within my being, to be able to succeed at the eleven plus examination. The plus was a new, green Raleigh bike, the downside a lifelong alienation from most of the kids on the estate with whom I had grown up. Oblivious to the nature of the ladder onto which I now stepped, I was then propelled a good few rungs upwards when I was streamed into the 'top' class out of five – 'the Latin stream' - in my second year. And there, at the bottom of a class of thirty, I took up my position for the next four years. Three times a year, end of term exams placed me at thirtieth out of thirty – for chemistry, French, English literature, Latin, biology, history and almost everything else. In the dark days before Christmas, in the new light of spring and in summer swelter, thirtieth out of thirty. Through 1960, 1961, the promise and threat from 1962 and the approaching cultural revolution signalled by 1963, thirtieth out of thirty. Term in and term out, year after year, for almost a third of my life. Number in class - thirty. Position in class – thirtieth.

By my first undergraduate year at Goldsmiths College, however, there were hints that I had sloughed off some or all of that

> *Wed 18th Jan 1967 - Physics lecture this*
> *morning brought a big surprise. With my*
> *combined physics marks I came joint top in the*
> *exam. Put me in an excellent mood*

*

I had no inkling of the career I was to follow after school and through my working life. Weak 'A'-level passes, but in the prestigious subjects physics and mathematics, had gained me a late September, last-minute place to study civil engineering at Woolwich Polytechnic in 1965. A grippingly lacklustre term then resulted in a first-opportunity exit that Christmas. The heady liberation of casual labour in the capital that followed, I knew, could only be a temporary experience.

By chance, a television documentary on changes in educational thinking and practice had caught my attention one evening while I was working as a porter on London Bridge Station. Children recognised as individuals. Gosh! Youngsters as innately curious and programmed to learn. Blimey! The pupil's interests as Education's starting point. How much further away could one get from the rotin', writin' an' 'rithmetickin' of my own schooldays? Creativity as the driver. I would have thrived on it. The teacher as producer and director of rich educational experiences and environments. What a privilege. Growing into a full and rounded person, intellectually sharp, artistically expressive and socially responsible. I wanted it for myself – and immediately.

At around the same time, in the year before my diaries began, I was hitchhiking back to London from Weymouth one Sunday evening and obtained a lift from a woman who was a primary school head teacher. The exact details of our location or conversation, like everything from before my first 1967 volume, is hazy but I do remember it being dark and her taking me as far as Camberley, Sunningdale, or one of those other affluent home counties towns straddled along the A30. Parking off the main road near her home we carried on whatever conversation we had been having although I really needed to be continuing my journey as nightfall would have rendered lifts less easily available. I must have been bemoaning my unwise choice of civil engineering as a course of study because, and this I do recall clearly, she asked whether I had considered a career in teaching. 'We need people like you in Education,' she said – the first careers advice, the first encouragement from a professional person, my first sense, really, of self-worth.

I subsequently applied to Goldsmiths College in New Cross to train as a secondary school English teacher. Their prospectus, on top of the inspirational television programme and my hitchhiking counsel, further quickened my ambitions. A particular paragraph seemed directed specifically at me, as if signalling covertly in the way that JD Salinger's books had once seemed to. Never mind the A level subjects you studied, it declared, teaching required a passion. There was no need to be constrained by exam choices made years earlier. Here was a chance to change tack if needs be and follow a more rewarding course.

I was invited for interview, and when I arrived I was directed to wait and informed that this would be with the Head of the Physics Department. I assumed this to be some continuation of the college's assertively cross-disciplinary stance and in just the same way some Literature Don would adjudicate on metaphors woven through the work of Newton, Kelvin and Einstein. The receptionist then informed me that each candidate would be required to first speak for one minute on a particular subject, handing me a folded slip of paper on which my topic was printed. Milton? Austen? Woolf or Eliot? I was finished. Passions meant pages and I was woefully unread. I unfolded the paper. 'You will be required to speak for one minute on …. ORBITS'.

Phew! There was a *deus ex machina* after all. I must have managed to extemporise satisfactorily, taking us both on a huge elliptical path through the icy silences of our solar system before drilling down into the atomic shell to reveal to us both the spectral wanderings of the electrons.

He told me to forget the English stuff. He would offer me, there and then, a place on a joint honours degree in physics and maths. It seemed to need an instant decision and my dreams of a long life of cultured reading were being held up to the light, be it wave or particle, and shown to be completely unsubstantial. He threw in a fourth-year postgraduate teaching certificate, as if a bargaining tool, and I accepted.

*

My first year at Goldsmiths College seems to reflect a comfortable blending of study and recreation, boosted by that early exam success in January

> *Fri 20th Jan 1967 - Morning – maths. Afternoon – hour or so with the log function. Afterwards an hour on the trampoline. After only three attempts I feel my technique is noticeably improving*

A written record here is extremely useful as my memory of the maths and physics degree that I was studying would almost certainly have been coloured, possibly obliterated, by the catastrophe of my finals a couple of years later. Entries scattered through '1967' do, in fact, reflect an engaged learner enjoying the intellectual fare on offer

> *Mon 13th Feb 1967 - (A problem set by our maths tutor) involved a differential equation and the second part asked how the solution 'might be used in the destruction of a suspension bridge by a patrol of girl guides'*
> *Thur 4th May 1967 - Physics practical this morning brought some rewards in the form of decent results for Hebb's method for the velocity of sound*

Psychology, my first-year subsidiary subject and still a rare and esoteric academic pursuit in those days, also generated enthusiasm

> *Fri 21st Apr 1967 - Became absorbed in (George)*
> *Miller's 'Psychology: The Science of Mental*
> *Life'. The more I read on this subject, the more I*
> *become fascinated by it*

The cracks in my sense of application, the balance tipping towards the social and physical, might, however, have begun appearing soon after my January exam success

> *Fri 3rd Feb 1967 - Arrived at college late and*
> *missed [Dr] Hails' lecture in order to go up to*
> *the bank. Finally perfected that [climbing] move*
> *on the wall after lunch. Worked in the library*
> *afterwards and arranged with Pete to meet him,*
> *Allison and Pru in the Prince Charles cinema,*
> *Leicester Square, at 7 o'clock*

Perhaps all the wonderful distractions of college life really did undermine my studies and it was as simple as a lack of hard work, despite my belief to the contrary, that put paid to my chances.

Or, maybe, a more longstanding problem was resurfacing particularly at the beginning of my final year?

> *Thur 3rd Oct 1968 - Today, lectures came back*
> *with a vengeance. B (maths tutor) set his usual*
> *impossible number of questions and I felt really*
> *sick and depressed by lunchtime. An afternoon*
> *in the physics lab was more interesting but*
> *living under pressure is going to be difficult*

I easily identified those I believed to be the cause of my torment and used my diary as a form of justification

> *Wed 8th Jan 1969 - My physics lecturers are*
> *ignorant men (except for B and N)*

In retrospect, and knowing what I now know, it is obvious that I lacked any appreciation of the concept of study skills, the fact that such procedures might exist let alone that they might be implemented to my benefit. Similarly, I possessed only a rudimentary awareness that examinations might be advantageously tackled by various strategic approaches.

Dreaminess, wandering interests and a lack of perseverance, I can all now accept as contributory factors. But there was also a long-standing pattern that had continued uninterrupted since my early teens in Weymouth. The assumption that application equalled deprivation. With my grammar school homework – in my house just uttering the term 'grammar school' seemed to warrant a hushed and reverential tone – I sat at the table in our otherwise rarely used, 'best' front room listening to the occasional shouts and laughter from neighbourhood children playing in the street. This was hard work, the absence of play. Conscientiousness was the denial of company and mischief. 'Just try to sit there for another quarter of an hour,' my mother might advise when my resentment mounted. 'You can't do better than your best,' if I complained that the requirements were beyond my understanding or capabilities. Any period not at the Swings, out across the Fields or down at the Fair, but spent instead in our front room in the presence of school books counted as 'revision', my full and only understanding of exam preparation. 'I should give it a rest now if I were you or you'll go straining your eyes,' she would eventually say

> *Tue 12th Nov 1968 - I'm sitting here over my books this evening and feeling really depressed. It's a sort of listless apathy. Kathy* [my

girlfriend] *tells me I've changed and I know it. I worry and take things too seriously*

The inescapability of my final exams, I suspect now, was driving me back into a deeply-rooted set of beliefs, whereby I genuinely believed I was giving it my best shot

Wed 8th Jan 1969 - I'm staying here for the weekday evenings in hall [instead of being with my girlfriend] *which is a drag but necessary*

I was not, however, without bouts of optimism at this stage despite my worries

Wed 8th Jan 1969 - I understand hydrodynamics and am now showing off wildly ... I have a new enthusiasm for my work – utilising as much time as possible

Something, however, must have shifted as the year turned away from winter and fell fondly into summer. I recorded nothing further about my exam preparation but I do remember writing out various mathematical proofs regularly, confident that at least one would spring from the page as I obeyed the invigilator's instruction and turned over my paper. And there it was! An offer, a gift, bright and unambiguous. A clutch of marks immediately secured! Just repeat the sequence of squiggles one more time, relive those regular evenings under the Anglepoise lamp, recreate by rote the abstract argument.

But as soon as I began, lines slipped from my grip or wandered in from other calculations. Axioms struggled for primacy in the opening lines. 'Given ...' failed to fix the focus. 'Therefore ...' lost its logic. I told myself, in mounting fury, that I had written out this proof without mishap once a fortnight since

January, crossed out another set of fickle formulae, and began again.

The whole three hours disappeared into caverns. I burrowed further from the light and air, deeper into despair. And when I finally re-emerged, dazed and blinking, back into the afternoon, I knew the world had darkened in my absence. However bland the diary entry I made some days later, I knew that some routes and pathways had been blocked to me and other destinations had become more inevitable

> Sun 22nd Jun 1969 - The days became very hazy and blurred. The exams came and went. I find it very hard to make any evaluation of my chances. Leave it

*

University courses, programmes of study, textbooks and examinations – in 1967, as now, these were the official vehicles of education and self-improvement. But on the street, in the crowd and down among the disinclined and disenchanted, a fermenting and pervasive agitation prevailed. Knowledge, beliefs and lived experience were hurled across barricades between escalating factions in their night-long battles for ascendancy.

Or, to be less grandiose, formal studies for me constituted only one part of the intellectual quest that I had somehow embarked upon a few years earlier. A far more important aspect, one that seemed to grab at me and demand an urgent response, was the drive towards conversation, the seeking out of an ever-widening circle of individuals who might illuminate my world with new opinions and further understandings

*Thur 4th May 1967 - Just planning an early
night when Dave A walked in and we talked for
about an hour and a half, with conversation
covering science fiction, DH Lawrence,
Chesterton and Steinbeck
Tue 7th Feb 1967 - Had coffee with Chris and we
talked about clichés, purposes in life, the
meaning of symbols
Thur 16th Feb 1967 - The talk – Christianity,
beatniks, poetry, fathers, lasted till after two in
the morning*

Adolescent posturing? A comical or pretentious list disguising a lack of depth and rigour? Awkward lunges towards a sense of identity? Or, a sustained bout of sublimation while stuck without a girlfriend during my first year at college?

Despite all the words, my diaries do not furnish the type of information that would allow me to answer these charges. My memory, stretching now over a ragged and fraying mesh of associations, is of a genuine and questioning search. But memory can be a notorious self-serving device.

I do know that, at college, I was merely continuing a process of challenge and exchange that had originated back in Weymouth a few years before and which continued on visits home

*Fri 24th Mar 1967 - (Weymouth) A walk home
during which John H explains the Greek 'golden
ratio' for a rectangle... Later in town met Ned,
John C and Bernie. We had a couple in the
King's Arms and began talking mathematical
philosophy. After closing time... subject
switches to education. Then coffee... where John
(most garrulous tonight) explains the philosophy*

of Berkeley and then the distinction between man and the animals. Home about 2.30

More useful for me in attempting now to know the value of our disquisitions are the rarer occasions when I attempted to record what was said and by whom. On one occasion this is laid out almost as minutes of a meeting, long before I had any real experience of such documents

Sat 15th Apr 1967 - (Weymouth) A very enjoyable conversation – 1) War - Roger has changed from complete pacifism to fighting if he felt the moral need. 2) Christianity - does a Christian know he will go to heaven? Martin says 'no'. 3) Marriage – Ivan speaks well on interdependence of husband and wife. 4) X [mutual but absent acquaintance] *– that he is a little immature and does not face reality. I cannot agree at all. Lift home from Martin at 3.30(am)*

As well as lists of subjects and occasional ventures into points of view, some entries include more direct appraisals of my companions themselves

Sun 22nd Jan 1967 - Ended up talking of sex and then films with Pete ... Pete tends to be a bit of an intellectual snob on jazz and films unfortunately

Weds 14th Jun 1967 - Spent three hours tonight talking to Adrian C. I had a completely incorrect impression of him. He is ... dedicated to teaching and we spent a great deal of time discussing creative writing in children, something which proved very successful in his last teaching practice. He showed me a 13-page letter from his tutor about one child's poem. With this sort of person in authority, there is hope

> *Mon 26th Jun 1967 - Spent a long time talking to*
> *Mark tonight ... his knowledge of Hindu and*
> *Buddhist thought is very good ... almost 7 hours*
> *interesting conversation this evening*

A cynical take on all this would be to identify the hours that might have been applied to my proper studies instead of being frittered away on idle chat.

But, nostalgic, sentimental and self-aggrandising though they may be judged, those years of conversations helped make me. I accept their earnestness and the youthful overstatement but still hold tight to these missives to myself from myself and a now vanished world.

*

Away from the intensity, perhaps to some, the pretentiousness, of this junior common room chatter, I was also gorging on conversation and the precarious excitement of shifting horizons presented by hitchhiking. Whereas my usual companions might be reasonably predictable, the topics that arose in strangers' cars, lorries and vans sprung up vigorously and unforeseen

> *Tue 5th May 1969 - Interesting lift from*
> *Dorchester to Bournemouth from an anti-*
> *establishment guy who spoke intelligently and*
> *sensitively and then revealed himself to be a*
> *retired army officer! The last lift, a lorry to*
> *Croydon, was driven by a guy who worked on oil*
> *rigs in the Middle East. He had also been on the*
> *N Sea rigs and reckons that last year one of the*
> *crew was bumped off without the news breaking*
> *out*

I revelled in the experiences and opinions of those who offered me lifts, aware then that my life could not otherwise have provided opportunities for such a range. Aware now that it never has to such a degree again

> *Fri 16th Jun 1967 - Tube to Hendon Central. Lift up the M1 in a very slow lorry. We were forced up onto the pavement at one stage by a drunken lorry driver – very precarious*
>
> *Wed 15th Mar 1967 – After tutorial this morning I went to see Dr Michael Hudson-Evans (I think) who is the consultant doctor to the college, also a chest specialist at Dartford Hospital. He gave me a lift around the S Circular the January before last when I was (hitch hiking) round to visit Martin and Roger in Battersea. We had a short chat about climbing and how I was getting on*

Although thumbing lifts as a student allowed me to travel, my first ventures a few years earlier had been borne of a less functional imperative. Jack Kerouac in his books had infused the activity with layers of sacramental significance – the surrendering of control, the pretext for, and experience of, the generosity of strangers. A Zen-like acceptance of life's unpredictability. Chuck in a heady mix of hard travellin' from W.H. Hudson, Walt Whitman or Bob Dylan, and I was at the roadside in my middle teens travelling from A to B and then straight back again solely for the 'spiritual' experience.

Hitchhiking at that time gained the approval of a diametrically opposite social order. The military were sometimes to be found launching initiative tests for their personnel, directing them to make their way to Gibraltar on half a crown or whatnot. My father also talked about thumbing lifts in Canada during the war, his RAF uniform always a sure asset he reckoned

> *Sun 12th Feb 1967 - Lift from there (Salisbury)*
> *to Guildford. Driver was talkative, a moustached*
> *army officer who had worked for some years*
> *surveying in Borneo. Interesting chat, I hardly*
> *noticed the miles*

My early diaries are an incidental account of an era more trusting and kind than those that have followed. I encountered no drivers who made me feel threatened and only a few whose company might have been a little unsettling

> *Sat 6th Apr 1967 - Hung about a bit in Sheffield*
> *until a guy took us, out of his way, to Bakewell –*
> *"We used to go on these holidays when we were*
> *young. Good, clean holidays they were, no sex or*
> *any of that"*

I do remember my knee being squeezed once somewhere over Salisbury Plain but my immediately frozen demeanour must have successfully signalled that I had no wish to advance the encounter. We had no knowledge then, as a society, of the lost buried under floorboards or sealed beneath a concrete patio.

These journeys sometimes yielded vicarious careers advice

> *Fri 31st Mar 1967 - Chepstow, I found a*
> *beautiful town. Weather glorious all day. A long*
> *wait there and finally a lift at about 1 o'clock*
> *from a civil engineer. "Take my advice, don't go*
> *out teaching, go into civils". "More money".*
> *Money, money …*

His comments were the result of my switch a year or so previously, away from his line of work and towards that of his wife. And, although I had no inkling then that most of my working life would be spent as a psychologist, that area of study did pop up during several rides

*Fri 19th May 1967 - A lorry then to Ringwood
(from Southampton). A very interesting chap.
My ears picked up when he said, sincerely,
'Money isn't everything'. We talked about the
advances in psychology and education, the
historical books that he read and poetry. A really
refreshing conversation
Mon 20th Mar 1967 - We left Weymouth about
10.30 ... Only a short wait for a lift to
Dorchester – a lecturer from South Dorset Tech
– "Have you boys ever heard of the Mormon
Church?"15 minutes then a lift to Plymouth ...
Driver had taken a degree in psychology – "It's
all a bloody load of crap really"- and was now a
travelling salesman for Brobat*

Sometimes the talk was less functional,
opinionated or combative and just delighted out of
its sheer battiness

*Fri 10th Feb 1967 - (Basingstoke) ... after three
or four minutes I got a lift from an affected but
rather likeable 'country' woman with a dog in
the front. The dog wasn't going to have any
puppies in the summer. They'd taken her to a
stud dog but no result even though "she loved
Tommy terribly dearly"*

And on other occasions the sheer exhilaration of
covering such distances outweighed the other
benefits of company and conversation

*Sat 8th Apr 1967 - (Llangollen) A long (one and
a half hour) wait in cold rain then a short lift. A
few minutes then a chap gave me (another) lift.
We got talking and I found him to be a person
very similar to myself. He talked about Dylan
(Bob and Thomas) in a way I welcomed and had
not heard in a long time. He was a bank clerk ...*

by the name of Dewi. We parted company in a
little town called Llanwrtys Wells. Began what I
expected to be an 11 mile walk to Llandovery.
Lucky lift on that desolate road from a farmer
who trained sheep dogs. He'd sold one in
Australia for £300! Two lifts into the Brecon
Beacons then a very fast one to Monmouth – 'I
drive fast because it's too much trouble to change
gear'. Then lift on the back of a 350-something
half way down the Wye Valley. Walked over a
perfect hump-backed bridge ... and picked up an
open-topped Triumph Herald. Zooming down
the valley past Tintern Abbey ... across the
Severn Bridge, and right to Templemeads
Station

Fri 5th Apr 1968 - (Congleton) From there a
couple of short lifts and then a very slow lorry
across the moors to Buxton and on to Baslow.
Coming over the top of the moors in a blizzard I
saw two shepherds plodding through the snow
with long staffs and it made me think of the old
man harrowing clods in Hardy's poem 'In time
of the breaking of nations' for some reason.
Derbyshire is as beautiful as ever – it's a county
that doesn't seem to receive the recognition it
deserves. A lift from Baslow took me to the
outskirts of Sheffield and from there I walked
four miles, in a fantastically happy state,
through a snow storm to Kathy's house.... I met
her father who gave me a rather curt handshake
and how-do-you-do but received me remarkably
well considering the drowned rat appearance
that I wore

Sun 12th Feb 1967 - Lift from Guildford up the
A3 in an old crate. Next lift was from a TR4

which brought me right into London Bridge
Station. Marvellous, whizzing in through
Brixham [Brixton], Streatham, Clapham. Cup of
Bovril and cheese rolls at station cured my
shaking from cold. Fabulous old lady behind the
counter

Harsh lessons in patience and resignation, all the more powerful and lasting through being self-induced, shaped my character, I am sure, more effectively than any regime imposed by some designated authority

Good Friday 1968 - (Snowdonia) We were
finally ready to leave at about 11.30. .... We got
a lift in Capel Curig, waited there and then one
into Betwys-Y-Coed. And then it began. It had
taken us until 2 to get here and then the cars
began to roll by, full of stupid gawking tourists.
It got later and later and no-one looked like
stopping ... Eventually, at 5.30, an open-topped
car drew up and gave us a prayed-for lift of 50
miles to Whitchurch. The driver was a middle-
aged walker and climber .... A short lift and then
one through Stockport to Hyde. We huddled in a
shop doorway eating fish and chips and
watching the bawdy drunks roll out of the pub.
As we stood on a corner waiting for a lift I began
to think that we would have to sleep out. Then
we suddenly got a lift from a guy who told us we
were mistaken and that the main Sheffield road
was a couple of miles. He then ran out of petrol
but we soon got another lift which took us over
the Pennines and dropped us on the Yorks
Moors. The place was really desolate but after
less than half an hour the second car to come
along picked us up and brought us in to the

*outskirts of Sheffield. A quick lift across the city
left us with about half an hour to walk. And
finally we arrived – at 2am. It was like the
muddled sequences of a dream*

Freedom to fail.
Freedom to be.

*

In my first teaching post, I soon became friendly
with two young members of staff who had both
trained at Goldsmiths on the same course as me but
a year earlier. John had a psychology degree from
London and Isabel, philosophy from Cambridge.
And whilst there was plenty to occupy my time and
thoughts in the crash course in survival that can be
an introduction to teaching, a niggling resentment
about my lack of graduate status still rubbed away at
the friable edges to my optimism and commitment.
Whilst I did not judge myself intellectually superior
to my new friends and colleagues, I did nonetheless
feel myself to be their equal.

As I neared my second year in the school and my
thoughts turned towards a next move, I began to
contemplate undertaking a part-time degree in
psychology at Birkbeck College in London.
Somewhere along the way, I had met and been
inspired by one or two of their mature students,
hardened to a schedule of two evenings a week for
seven years, and had written to the University of
London to enquire whether my pass in psychology
after the first year of my original degree might
reduce my period of study from seven to six years

*Sat 6th May 1972 - Had a letter from London
University today saying that I would be credited
with three quarters of a degree. If I wished to take*

the remaining part as an external student. These
are new regulations. Feeling queasy again

The changed arrangements, in a time before the advent of the Open University, presented a massive opportunity to me, reducing the period I would have to study from seven years to two or three. And they informed me that I could, if I wished, pursue a course of private study and thus avoid having to register at Birkbeck and then make the long trek into London after work twice a week for a period equivalent to a quarter of my life up to that date. I am still enormously grateful to the unknown official who thought to explain these specific details as they applied to my untypical circumstances – it changed the course of my career and my life

Sun 21st May 1972 - John took me to Waterloo
station. On the journey we went through the
external London psychology syllabus and John is
very keen to help me with suggestions for
relevant books and lending me his notes

Others advised me that attempting an external degree solely by private study, untutored and with only a syllabus, reading lists and past exam papers as my guides, was an act of folly and doomed to fail. There were also hints that students on 'internal' degrees were taught by the very people who set the exam papers and that I would miss out on crucial hints, winks and emphases – the coded secrets of some covert, academic fellowship. But initial scans of my clutch of documents from the university suggested that a grasp of psychology would prove far less elusive than the higher reaches of differential calculus and Einstein's searchlight revelations.

I overcame my reservations and registered

> *Mon 19th Jun 1972 - Plan to reduce bulk of diary*
> *entries to allow for studying*
> *Tues 20th Jan 1972 - Find one and a half hours of*
> *studying per night possible. Don't know what*
> *else I used the time for ... Find reading has a*
> *more invigorating effect than a bath. Helps*
> *switch off the day*

The diaries record my satisfaction - no, the thrill of finding myself capable of sustained application – and the intrinsic interest the material itself held for me

> *Sun 2nd Jul 1967 - Sat in all day reading*
> *Broadbent. Was pleased to have set myself a high*
> *standard and to have achieved it by finishing the*
> *book*
> *Sun 16th Jul 1972 - A quiet day reading*
> *'Subcortical Mechanisms'. Sat in the garden this*
> *morning and indoors this afternoon and evening.*
> *Pleased with my apparent progress*

There are many similar entries, my motivation rushing onwards, through topics that both astonished me by their profundity and others that held me in less awe

> *Tue 29th Aug 1972 - Was reading some*
> *neurophysiology this morning and came across*
> *the incredible experiments of Krech, Rosenweig*
> *and Bennett. They found that the cortex of rats*
> *brought up in cages with toys and the company*
> *of other rats was up to 10% thicker and heavier*
> *than that of rats raised in isolation and in bare*
> *cages. It seems almost unbelievable that this*
> *should be so blatant and the human parallels are*
> *so obvious*
> *Tue 21st Nov 11 1972 - Read some more Cofer*
> *and Appley and I enjoyed it. I have been wading*
> *through the experimental investigations of*

*Hull's theory and have found it heavy going, but
it has taken so long because I am determined to
understand all the points*
*Sat 25th Nov 1972 - Picked up at the library and
started reading 'Attachment' by John Bowlby. I
have really been digging this book and although
it is on my reading list, I haven't been
underlining so as not to disturb my enjoyment*

In some ways, my diaries from this period serve as
first, abbreviated drafts of my study notes and this
continues in varying intensities up until my final
exams in the summer of 1974. Other aspects of my
personal and working life continue, of course, but in
an atmosphere of tightly and efficiently managed
time.

A move to South Yorkshire in 1973 was followed
quickly by the birth of our first son who, with some
embarrassment now, I find was quickly enrolled as a
living aid to my understanding of the more abstruse
aspects of some developmental psychology theories

*Sun 17th Jun 1973 - Ben seems to have reached
the second sub stage of Piaget's 'sensory motor'
period, that of 'primary circular reactions', for
what it's worth*
*Thur 16th Aug 1973 - I'm in the depths of an
essay on linguistic development in children and
am enjoying every moment of it*

On a conventional psychology degree at that time,
half a day a week would be spent on 'practical work'
devising and carrying out experiments in areas such
as perception, learning and memory. For somebody
undertaking 'private study' filling the required
experimental logbooks was a problem, partly
because the practical work had to be carried out
under the auspices of a qualified practitioner and

partly because specialised equipment was also sometimes required. London University had consequently devised an intensive summer school where it was possible to cram into a period of ten days the equivalent of one-years' worth of work. The course had a reputation, a fearsome one, for pace and pressure

> *Tue 24th July 1973 - The Experimental Psychology course at Birkbeck is going fantastically well. There is an incredible atmosphere of industry as everyone desperately tries to perform and write up 12 experiments for marking by the end. However, I have found the past two days very enjoyable, just eating, breathing and sleeping a subject*
> *Fri 3rd Aug 1973 - The end of my course. Utterly spent. I've never worked so hard in my life as these past two weeks and now seem to have caught flu as a consequence. It has been very stimulating working hard and I seem to have written up more experiments than anyone else (9) and these all have good grades. A mock practical (exam) I did yesterday came back with a B+. The course has given me a lot of confidence in my abilities, although I know that I always underachieve on important exams*

As my final year of study approached, somebody told me about the National Extension College, a correspondence course that provided a tutoring service up to and including degree level courses. I registered and climbed aboard another accelerated period of study

> *Sun 11th Nov 1973 - A new tutor from the NEC, who seems really helpful, has launched me into a well-planned scheme of essay writing and*

reading in cognitive psychology. This is taking up most of my spare time

My tutor was a PhD student from Sheffield who proved incredibly supportive, whose written comments on my essays almost equalled my own submissions in length. One time he suggested we met for a tutorial in a pub and once again I was heartened by his obvious commitment to my succeeding, by his efforts far in excess of his contractual obligations. What I realised as we talked, was that I was now reading contemporary research papers, waiting impatiently sometimes for studies *in press,* whereas with physics and mathematics the theories and experiments that had occupied me had usually been developed and performed in a former century, sometimes hundreds of years earlier. Although not of the same significance in the grander firmament of knowledge, of course, these contemporary investigations nonetheless delighted me as I peered alongside my mentor over minor precipices into the wells of our joint ignorance.

As the final exams loomed, I was almost relishing the adversarial contest with unseen question setters and markers. As if standing alone at the top of some rock pinnacle and belaying myself securely, I had a deep sense of mastery, an awareness of having been reliant solely on my own judgement and effort. Not over-confident, but not inwardly craven either, I felt at long last ready to give of my best

Thur 6th Jun 1974 - The long haul is nearly over. Last Monday I sat my practical paper at Birkbeck ... I had a bad night's sleep and dragged myself down Tottenham Court Road in the morning, desperately trying to wake up. I didn't do full justice to the paper, but I think I

did enough to get through. Today's [theory papers at Nottingham] *were much better. I didn't get one or two of the questions I really wanted, but, considering how much I have been on my own in this course, and have had to identify important areas myself, I was very pleased with the papers*

Back in some room in Nottingham city centre, where the small diaspora of London University's external students all came together, I took my final paper. I emerged afterwards knowing that I had performed well enough to pass my degree

Sat 22nd Jun 1974 - The exam papers went okay...

I could step into the future, confident at last and with a sure sense of direction

... I caught the wrong train from Nottingham, ended up in Loughborough, came back to Nottingham and then decided to hitch up the M1

8. THOSE WHO CAN'T

As my diaries commence in January 1967, I have been studying at Goldsmiths for a term, aged twenty, and living in Aberdeen Hall, an all-male residence up on the edge of Blackheath. More than a fish out of water, almost a beached whale, I was embarking on a three-year ethnographic experience, living intimately among a large tribe of trainee teachers but also tucked away at one remove among a very small group studying solely for a straightforward maths and physics degree. As the others in my hall were dreading the approach of their first teaching practices, I was in the laboratory measuring the wavelength of light using Newton's rings. While they dived into the philosophy, psychology and sociology of education, I struggled to keep afloat among the escalating abstractions of differential equations and 'functions of a complex variable'.

Among the student body in college, I fitted in, fitted out in flared denim jeans with paisley inserts, flip flops, collarless shirts, a neckerchief and shoulder-length hair. But back in my hall of residence, lines were drawn and 'standards' set

> *Tue 17th Jan 1967 - Hall meeting in evening, and how. A.D. stated that he was a member of Goldsmiths College, unfortunately, and did not want the place (hall) invaded by the riff-raff to be found in college*

Aberdeen Hall's 'Head Student' (A.D.) and the majority of my fellow residents were selected, I later learned, by virtue of having previously attended various public schools. In addition, a sizeable minority were training to become teachers of Physical Education. One of the lecturers who also lived there was an ex-pupil of Weymouth Grammar School and had selected me because of some perceived loyalty. There they all were marooned high on the edge of South London's open parkland, in cravats, jackets with leather arm patches, and clipped hairstyles like freshly-mown lawns, moaning about the seething dissolution down in the main body of Goldsmiths. As if from some isolated hill station, they lamented their loss of empire. *Mens sana in corpore sano.* A healthy male paranoia in a corporate mind

> *Sat 10th Jun 1967 - A.D. accused P.R. of eating too much food, at least taking it and not eating it, and politely informed him that it was not British manners. Whether one informs politely does not make up for the fact that what is informed is abominably impolite. The culprit is, anyway, a British citizen despite his Asian appearance ...*

(I had surely acquired that 'abominably' from them.)

> *... When A.D. was informed later that P.R. probably came from a more upper class home than he, he flew into a tantrum and screeched that he could trace his ancestry back to the Anglo-Saxons*

I could not have engineered a more revealing education into the collective insecurities of a creaking class system. Regular 'hall meetings' were called for which attendance was mandatory, a recurring discussion topic being the 'standards' of behaviour that should be expected from 'gentlemen'. While others 'down in college' danced until the small hours to the Bonzo Dog Doo Da Band or agitated for sit-in occupations, we were lectured on the correct manner in which cook should be addressed and the precise conditions under which gentlemen would be permitted to remove their jackets during dinner. The Summer of Love held at bay by the Old Order

> *Mon 17th Apr 1967 - Back at Hall in the evening a bottle of cider appeared on each table. Apparently this was in honour of the (old) committee handing over to the new. Toasting the Queen and the Aberdeen Angus and listening to the most banal of speeches*

It was Oxbridge to a tee – Oxbridge all bar the history, wit and erudition.

Fortunately, I found enough allies and external distractions to make this bizarre social experience bearable. I had a room tucked away at the top of the building and this added to my sense, one that I rather savoured at times, of being a stranger in a strange land. That these dull throw-backs could be contemplating taking over responsibility for nurturing a nation's malleable young minds was difficult to contemplate and one incident in particular gave me grave concerns.

In my second year, and I find that I had made no record of this incident in my diary, a student named Terry was overwhelmed by a sudden religious conversion. Although I did not know him well, I seemed to find myself sitting next to him at mealtimes at some table or other well to the periphery of the central core of rugger-and-order types.

'Don't you see, Jesus is my saviour!' announced Terry during tea one day, wild with a sense of martyred isolation and scanning the faces opposite him.

'He died for me. Don't you get it?' he persisted, flecks of saliva at the sides of his mouth, hurt driving his restless gaze.

'Terry,' I fumbled, 'probably best not to –'

'He died for you as well. All of you!'

That night they boxed him into one of the tiny kitchens. Fists smacked the zealot's face and his body as it folded. Jeers from the giants of the gym, solid lessons not to be soon forgotten delivered by the track-suited. Supplementary spite and bile from the woodworkers.

I had no means of challenging the mob.

I felt a deep unease about the classrooms of the future.

*

Future careers, though, were easily assigned to what seemed their rightful place – the future. I had a degree to pass, climbs to climb, books to read, poems to write, films to watch and discuss. And discuss some more. The Debating Society. Holiday jobs. Friends. Politics to puzzle over. Music to muse over. And I even descended to the level of the Caving Club at times. I had a girlfriend, subsequently a fiancée, then a wife.

My diaries, daily through most of 1967 and then 'as and when' for my next two college years, are filled with the fizz and pace of all of this. But, not mentioned, is any sense of serious planning for my future employment.

One idea bloomed briefly in the summer of 1968, a year before my degree finals, and I see it first expressed after a totally unexpected encounter in Piccadilly Circus

> *Sun 4th Aug 1968 - (We) wandered back to Leicester Square looking for a pub. Suddenly I thought I recognised a guy who was selling International Times. It was a chap called Steve D, who had been the year below me at school back in Weymouth, but was now camouflaged behind bright 'hippy' clothes and hair. He took us along to a pub in Piccadilly Circus, where there was quite a little beat scene going. At first I felt out of place - almost frightened although I didn't like to admit it - but I soon was able to relax ... Kathy also became aware of the unpretentious atmosphere amongst these people, and this enjoyable evening only served to reinforce my ambition to set up a mountain school for recreation and philosophising*

This little band of innocents were planning to live communally somewhere in wildest Wales and I was charmed by their determination and a little upstaged by what seemed like an easily shared and genuine commitment on their part. A couple of weeks later these thoughts were still with me

> *Sat 17th Aug 1968 – My friends now leaving college all seem unsure of what they wish to do and are questioning whether they want to fill the social roles for which they have been trained... I talked again with Martin on the beach and he is feeling more and more the need to break away from a dull life. The idea of a mountain school appeals to him and Rob made wise suggestions about trying for sponsorship*

As well as, obviously, combining what I felt to be my educational vocation with my enthusiasm for climbing, such an ambition would allow me to live in the mountains, an idea that seemed increasingly attractive. In addition, I envisaged such a school would cater specifically for young people who experienced difficulties and caused trouble in school. The character-building nature of mountain adventure, a notion I managed to somehow both scorn and at the same time subscribe to, had a deep resonance. My early climbing mentor, the Revd. Bob, had put his climbing rope where his religious convictions were, and introduced ex-convicts and other tough guys to the discipline and heady dangers of ascent.

My vague aspiration to repeat and extend such an approach bore, at that age and in those times, no consideration of the practical, professional and financial implications and, as far as the record of my diaries indicates, soon melted away.

Not so for Andy, my friend and main climbing partner, who after college worked as an outdoor pursuits instructor on a casual basis for various bodies before landing a permanent such post with Edinburgh Education Authority. What seemed like a plum job, freed from the more humdrum and tedious parts of a teacher's role, turned however in a short time to one that brought horror and tragedy right up to, and inside, his own front door

> *Mon 22nd Nov 1971 - Main national news today is the deaths of five of a group of seven Edinburgh school pupils in a blizzard in the Cairngorms. One of the boys was found alive and also the 20-year old girl who was leading them. Her name was Cathy and in the photo on the television news she looked like the Cathy who works with and lives in the flat with Andy*

Britain's worst mountaineering disaster resulted in major changes in outdoor education in general as well as disillusion for my friend

> *Weds 26th Jan 1972 - Talking to (Andy)*
> *Handford on the phone. Later he tells me that the*
> *enquiry on the Cairngorms disaster last year is*
> *to take place on February 8. He says that people*
> *have stopped thinking about the kids who have*
> *died and a political tussle has taken precedence*

As well as encouraging me, as tragedies always did, to think again about my degree of commitment to mountaineering, this awful event helped consolidate a vague notion I had that there were good reasons for keeping one's main employment separate from activities that provided relaxation, variety or escape.

*

As my third year was coming to an end, I attended a presentation by the college's organiser for its post graduate course in primary education. Len Marsh could hold an audience in a way that the scientists and mathematicians who had been lecturing me for three years could not begin to duplicate (let alone replicate to 'n' recurring).

He presented a mesmerising account of children's learning and the crucial role played by teachers as adjuncts and guides to this process. My original intentions were re-awakened and I signed up immediately. Despite my excitement, and no doubt because my final degree examinations were looming not far off, my diaries contain fewer entries at around this time and none about this significant decision.

The crushing blow of my failed degree was offset by the college's decision to honour their original offer to me and allow me to undertake the one-year teacher training course. In retrospect, the enthusiasm with which I launched into this new course was probably fuelled in part by a desire to put behind myself this latest and huge academic failure. Nonetheless, despite many pages filled with my usual topics, the very first comment on my new sense of direction does not come until well into the autumn term

> *Sun 5th Oct 1969 - I'm just planning to face another week in school at Gravesend. The past one has been really enjoyable despite the long journeys on the bike*

The following thin stream of entries again concerns itself with describing climbing weekends away, news of friends and continuing soliloquies about, well, the purpose of life really. My only other mention that term of this training course, which I remember as highly stimulating and refreshing with a new bunch of graduate students from a wide range of academic backgrounds and locations, was a brief note about a familiarisation visit to a school in Catford where I was to undertake a teaching practice later in the Spring term

> *Tues 8th Dec 1969 - I went down to D [school] to look over the place, and the fears that I had had after the build-up were pretty well allayed*

Not much to show for a period in which I remember becoming a proselytiser for 'progressive primary education'

> *Tues 29th Jan 1970 - This diary has ceased to become at all representational ... I've started my T.P. [Teaching Practice] which should lead to a few pages of 'critical self-analysis' but it doesn't.*

It now becomes just a series of moments and impressions

Perhaps, my college course was requiring me to keep far more of a written record of my thoughts and experiences thus obviating the need for a diary to fulfil the same purpose? Our course combined stimulating presentations from both academics and practising teachers, visits that even included a day trip on a Saturday all the way to a school in West Yorkshire to meet with some of its staff. We experienced art with a tutor who encouraged us to break loose from our academic mindsets, to paint our feet if we wished to walk across long rolls of paper, to do the same with a bicycle if we preferred!

Instead of writing anything about this iconoclastic excitement, my diary seemed to emphasise a mood of despondency. Disengagement almost

Fri 28th Feb 1970 - The thought of a job next term is bringing us down a bit. The whole idea of doing the same thing in the same place day after day frightens me, even though I really like primary teaching. The idea of having to have interviews all over the place during the Easter holidays and thereby messing up a stretch of time which could be used for a good bit of climbing is a bit of a drag

Thur 12th Mar 1970 - A real malaise has been hanging around for weeks now, a sort of boredom and non-involvement with everything. Today the warm weather has come and cleared things up a little. I think perhaps I have been trying to give my whole to primary education

Reading this volume again nearly fifty years later, the reason for this sag in optimism and motivation is obvious. On the very same pages

Fri 28th Feb 1970 - Jan flew out of Heathrow
airport on her way to a two-and-a-half- year
teaching post in the Falklands Islands
Thur 12th Mar 1970 - Lots of letters came today.
There was a card from Mark from a base in the
Antarctic. It is quite amazing to receive almost
irrefutable evidence that Antarctica exists

I was using my diary, not to record my new adventures as an idealistic young teacher to be, but as a place to lament a way of life and a community of friends, that was ending.

*

The dozen or so students on my course were encouraged to feel part of a movement that was revolutionising primary school education. Lady Plowden, with the ink barely dry on the influential report by her committee, visited and spoke to us, approving of our implementation of the 'child-centred' and modernising philosophy her committee espoused. I made no mention. Strong links were strengthened with certain schools and a handful of local authorities by encouraging us students to apply for their vacancies in order to build up critical masses of supposedly like-minded people who were able to support and motivate each other. I was both flattered to be granted membership of this zealous community - to belong - and, at the same time, suffered some nagging discomfort about the ease with which such attitudes might tip into exclusivity and complacency.

I remember many lengthy debates with my fellow course members about such matters but, again, made no record. Perhaps I was talked-out on those increasingly infrequent occasions when I did open my diary. At least I noted my appointment to a post in a school favoured by my course – and also a contrasting, but probably half-hearted, last attempt to resist a career route that felt somehow too prescribed

> *Thur 14th May 1970 - I've also been lucky enough to get a job for next year at Y School in Amersham after trying for one in Newfoundland. I'm really looking forward to starting it but I shall be interested to see whether I can survive the routine easily*

Then, there is nothing more on this matter until

> *Wed 22nd Sept 1970 - Been teaching 3 weeks now. Enjoying it. I'm not sure of my philosophy but the everyday procedure itself is pleasant. Tonight I had the first session with one of my fathers who cannot read. I think we will succeed. I have a strong feeling of vocation doing this, I hope it's not just self-importance*

Instead, I record a little about the Isle of Wight Festival, mountain ascents in the wet and cold of Snowdonia over half term and phone calls to, and news from, friends

> *... Maggie is now au-pairing in Paris*

And then, the first term is over. In reflective mood, I am aware that I am failing to capture any sense of the new life I am living and make the decision to revert to a more disciplined and detailed approach

> *Boxing Day 1970 - There seems little point in these retrospective diaries as they lack any form of substance because of the wide time span they attempt itemise in so short a number of words. So I've decided to go back to a 'day-to-day' diary in the hope that more trivial items reflect the priorities/obsessions of whatever time and place I am in*

There are smudges of ink – real ink from a reloadable fountain pen – on the red marbled-effect cover of '1971'. Inside, for the first four months, each day is recorded in a beautifully executed italic script after which I revert to various biros but with the neatness maintained. It is the most carefully crafted of all my volumes, its mode of presentation reflecting major precepts of the educational methods to which I was wedded – the creation of attractive artefacts, a considered and thoughtful approach and a pride in one's achievements.

Major work-focused themes in this volume, written long before the days of a government-prescribed national curriculum, were concerns about what to teach, how to do so, and for what aim or purpose? More accurately though, the emphasis was placed upon the recipients of these efforts - how, why and to what end did they learn? Many pages from this period, one in which individual teachers were by and large expected to resolve these weighty issues for themselves in their own classrooms, reflect a continuing engagement with such matters.

When these struggles seemed to be without end or resolution, I was encouraged by the number of visitors who came to witness our methods. In some weeks streams of students, teachers and educational administrators proceeded through our corridors and loitered within our classrooms. The effects were double-edged, a sense that we were delivering a style of education novel and interesting enough to attract a range of visitors could be offset by feelings of being disrupted and overwhelmed.

Sometimes it was trainee teachers and their tutors

Fri 17th Mar 1972 - A group of Bulmershe
[teacher training college] *mature students
came around the school and they must have got a
good impression*
*Thurs 4th Mar 1971 - A hideous day at school.
The children were terribly behaved ... we had 25
students from Goldsmiths*

At other times, practising teachers whose positive
judgements provided some validation for me when
my own sense of what we were accomplishing
experienced a wobble

*Fri 19th Mar 1971 - Visitors again today put an
end to a week of very unpleasant tensions. These
people were very nice – two teachers – and they
commented that school had a very happy and
enthusiastic atmosphere. I wish I could decide to
what extent this is illusory. I certainly had that
impression when I came here last term*
*Wed 10th Feb 1971 - There was a group of
visiting teachers from Tower Hill today, among
whom was an American woman who said she
would let me know if she could find me any
contacts about a job in the States in the near
future*

My desire to be somewhere else, anywhere far
away and therefore, *de facto*, more glamorous
obviously persisted even if only at the level of
grasping at vague opportunities as they scurried past

*Thur 18th Mar 1971 - Today provided quite a bit
of gloom – wet playtimes and visitors. The boss
tried to get everybody interested in Miss D, who
was an authority on children's books. The
American visitors, after a bit of chatting up, took
my name and said they'd send me the blurb
about their school in Richmond, Virginia*

Complimentary head teachers were, of course, an additional source of encouragement

> *Tue 22nd Feb 1972 - A nice day. We had a visit from the Plowden group who were quite innocuous. It was good to see Len Marsh again. I find him a very inspiring guy. It is easy to forget the postgrad year and think that Marsh is only about drawing pots of flowers, whereas he is really a very aware person thinking about the whole nature of education in our society*
> *Wed 7th Jun 1972 - A non-descript day. A group of heads on the same course as P* [colleague] *came around today. Was able to leave the class with Noelle* [8-yr old pupil] *playing the guitar and the others singing*

I am sure there was a party of Japanese visitors but my diaries suggest otherwise unless they came in my first term. The record does however remind me of many others whose presence I would otherwise be definitely unable to recall

> *Tue 5th Dec 1972 - We got to school to find that the Plowden group who we were expecting tomorrow were arriving today instead. It was dark and raining and a feeling of disaster in the air. The day started with a lecture by somebody from the Commonwealth Institute, which was pretty boring. Len spent quite a bit of the day in my room and I heard him talking to a headmaster, fingers splayed in gesture, about the 'quiet purposefulness' in the room. The kids themselves were good ... I notice (their) growing confidence and independence*

Looking back, I wonder about the sense of irritation that these visitations sometimes provoked in me

> *Mon 8th Mar 1971 - The boss says that the expected 6 Americans turned out to be 25 in a coach! That gastroenteritis couldn't have come at a better time!*

A major event in my first year of teaching was the interest shown in our school by a flagship television science programme, my excitement almost displaced in my diary by cynicism about the degree of disruption – and pretence – that would be occasioned

> *Mon 7th Jun 1971 - BBC 2's Horizon programme wants to use our school for part of a programme, specifically, music, and so the greatest show on earth is once again in action*

As a science programme, Horizon was particularly interested in the ways in which developments in psychology, cognitive theory and linguistics were influencing educational practice in some schools

> *Tue 15th Jun 1971 - The Horizon team arrived today ... It soon transpired that they didn't really want to hear what our school wanted to do but ... impose their own structure. They seemed quite aware and Morris was reduced to the side lines along with W and N. I just couldn't curb my bouts of cynicism, although I feel I shouldn't let it bother me*
>
> *Wed 16th Jun 1971 - One of the most, probably the most, depressing day at school. Morris was in a flurry of vanity with the BBC still here. He kept sending around notes and coming and telling the kids to be quiet. They are as sick of the show as I am.*

The most striking feature about my many work-related entries from this period though, and my biggest regret about them, is that I said so little about the educational activities that I and my other colleagues arranged and delivered. These constant visitors came for a reason but it was my frustrations with my boss and other senior colleagues that I chose to preserve – either a real missed opportunity or an accurate reflection of the stresses and strains of a first teaching post. The peculiar and close juxtaposition of high-mindedness and pettiness may be just a personal aberration coming to the fore in that time and place, or it may be a more general comment about the nature of that 'child-centred' educational world.

Instead, I wish now that I had kept more notes - any notes, in fact, - about logic games that I invented for some of my mathematically-ablest eight year olds. Using sets of commercially available plastic shapes in various sizes and colours we explored, with increasing degrees of abstraction, general principles behind 'transformations'. So, taking a small green triangle, for example, and taking it through one change could result in a large green triangle or a small, yellow triangle or a number of other options. We invented our own notation for describing these various manoeuvres and for some children these various activities constituted the limit of their capabilities.

But with the most able *in this respect* it was possible to dispense with the actual objects themselves and create and explore together, and sometimes solve, questions and puzzles in purely written form – a precursor to our own advanced form of algebra.

On another occasion, we created, as a whole class, a piece of 'music' composed from the range of sounds to be heard in a school playground. Skipping chants, with an actual rope striking the ground on each rotation, set a beat upon which additional, contrasting rhythms were gradually superimposed. Other chants and sounds, all suggested by the children, were added to create a crescendo and then stripped out again to form a diminution. The challenge then was to find some graphic form with which to record this composition, another form of notation which involved a long strip of plain wallpaper and which illustrated many of the features of conventional musical notation. The classroom layout and the lack of fixed subject periods allowed a style of coming together as a whole group to discuss options for developing the overall task I had set, then dispersing into smaller working groups to pursue various aspects before reconvening to pool ideas and generate the next set of tasks.

I regret recording so few of these activities in any detail. Instead of the back-biting and staffroom quarrels, this was the arena that required and developed creativity, problem solving, collaboration and intellectual stimulation – both for the kids and for myself. We performed this 'musical' composition for parents and the rest of the school, carefully following the huge score draped across the assembly hall. But my entry is brief and insubstantial

> *Thur 18th May 1972 - Our class did an assembly today and it really gave me, and I think them, a big kick*

Despite my complaints about 'the boss', I felt valued and appreciated by him, secure enough, I suppose, to be able to voice my criticisms directly to him at times

> *Wed 16th Jun 1971 - Spent some time talking to the boss tonight and he allowed me to speak a lot*

of my mind. I said the staff room discussion was
so limited, partly because it was dominated by
him. I also suggested that more experienced
teachers in our school seemed a little insensitive
... I shall have to keep quiet for a few days now

Looking back over the decades and from a position of greater self-awareness, I can recognise how much I was having to manage my contradictory feelings about an older, male authority figure – in large part, perhaps, projections and transference from my father

Bank Holiday Monday Aug 1971 - I went in (to
school) at lunchtime. The boss looked bad. He
went home ... complaining of pains across his
chest all day and being sick in the morning. His
face was white and covered with sweat. It has
always been thought that he's an ideal candidate
for heart trouble. If this is what this is then it
will be difficult for him to slow down. It seems
likely that he will have to be off for a while to
rest, but he's a tough old bastard
Sun 12th Sept 1971 - Went into school this
morning. The boss is complaining of feeling tired
and puts this down to not having had a holiday.
He said he would have had one but couldn't see
the point

Helpless, not knowing how to intervene nor whether I had any right to do so, I said nothing. My diary entries almost reveal a frisson of melodrama, as if I was at last entering the adult world, for real this time with no turning back. And, I suspect, still unable to truly believe that people do actually die, the deaths of my two grandfathers having been tucked skilfully out of sight by my parents during my growing up.

I was away with my class at a nearby residential centre when I was called to the phone and my denial or unworldliness or whatever it was, crumbled

Wed 3rd Nov 1971 - Kathy phoned me tonight to tell me that Mr Morris had died at his home at about 7.30 this evening. Apart from grandparents this is the closest I have been to somebody who has died. I think he knew it would happen if he didn't stop working and he preferred to keep working. A strange guy – very often I found he upset me and yet in those few times that we chatted quietly together, he came across as a person so young at heart

Tue 9th Nov 1971 - It was the funeral this afternoon. The service I found very moving and it hit me very forcibly just how hard he had worked for kids and I remembered how interested he was in them. He liked to be rewarded with praise for his efforts by visitors but that doesn't negate his tremendous effort. I remember how much help and encouragement he gave me, and it is fairly apparent that we need him

I was twenty-five at the time and, although I did not write it I my diary, I consoled myself with the thought that 'the boss had had a good innings'.

He had died, I seem now to recall, somewhere in his late forties.

9. NORTH

Mon 22nd May 1972 - A warm day. Took it easy pressing shirts and John's three-piece suit and walked down the main street with Val. The station at Bridport was all boarded up and overgrown with weeds and yet there on the platform was a one-coach train. A conductor came through the carriage to collect the fares from the five passengers. Stepped out at Maiden Newton. Wandered around searching for public transport or a taxi. A kindly country lady invited me into her house to use her telephone and discovered there was a coach which went to Evershot. On the coach was another girl going to the interview

If I were to throw away my diaries it would be the record of moments and incidental events like this that I would miss the most. Without them I would not otherwise have remembered feeling energised by the new, slip-on identity provided by a friend's suit, staying the night before with old friends, travelling in the last doomed days along a rural branch line or the country kindness of a stranger.

But the interview itself, for a teaching post in West Dorset, requires no written account. It was a decisive event and has remained crystal clear in my recall through the years.

*

After the death of my first head teacher in November 1971, I witnessed our staff room degenerate into gossip and anxiety surrounding the appointment of his successor. Suddenly, the main reason for living in the home county heartlands, in expensive and highly conservative Amersham, had disappeared. I witnessed an organisation, its leader dead for less than a week, turn inwards upon itself in petty disarray

> *Mon 8th Nov 1971 - Bitter struggles among the staff seem to be going on. CB seems to have come out very strongly against AS which all seems a bit unnecessary and, in fact, very unpleasant so soon after the boss's death*

Diaries can lay out the daily drip of dilemmas and unresolved decisions. As the world turned from the exuberant innocence of the 1960s, my friends and I, my generation in fact, felt our adolescence slipping away behind us. In years when the country recoiled from sobering slaps of industrial unrest, inflation and a violent hike in the price of oil, my entries reveal me to be spinning around, unable to decide in which direction to face the future

> *Tue 15th Jun 1971 - We decided in the car coming home, to move to Derbyshire after another year here and then go to Dorset afterwards. I want to go to Dorset to settle eventually but I don't want to exhaust my moves too soon*
>
> *Sun 5th Sep 1971 - Lately I have been thinking constantly of going to India next year*
>
> *Sat 11th Sep 1971 - I wouldn't mind settling to wistfulness on Portland one day*

Within a week, I could relocate my focus from spiritually fashionable India to a stubborn lump of limestone jutting out into the English Channel. Without a diary, memory would almost certainly have smoothed these dreams and fancies into a far less erratic process, and certainly not one in which my ambitions could switch direction even within a twenty-four-hour period. The effects on others, particularly my wife, might also have been tucked away into some tidy corner by the persistent efforts of forgetfulness

> *Sun 28th Nov 1971 - Kathy says that she can't keep up with my changing ambitions*

Pages spell out contradictory pulls exerted in part by the continuingly changing, continental mosaic revealed in letters from old friends in new locations

> *Fri 17th Sep 1971 - (John S) tells me that there was an article on English hippies abroad in the Daily Mirror during the summer and there was a close-up picture and few lines on Maggie. She was apparently in Kabul in Afghanistan*
>
> *Weds 22nd Sep 1971 - Isabel* [friend and colleague] *and I sat talking about getting in and out of ruts ... I think of Maggie in Afghanistan, Mark in Antarctica, Jan in the Falklands and Martin L in Nepal. I suppose there will come a day when all my friends are settled and then the wanderlust won't nag so much because it will seem impossible to satisfy*

Until our friend, Jan, took up her teaching post in the Falkland Islands, nobody I knew had ever flown. Except for the very rich or those with esoteric employment providing a plane ticket, travel involved hitchhiking, buses or, in one or two cases, ship. Beyond the boundary of western Europe, transport became the stuff of myths and legend. Once over the Bosphorus the trail went cold, the signal died and people disappeared. No transport timetables to consult in advance, no telephones with which to maintain contact, no flights back home if the zeal fizzled out. Only letters, weeks out of date by the

time they fell onto our doormat with an exotic
flourish

> *Fri 15th Oct 1971 - A letter… from Al Spencer*
> *saying that he went out to Afghanistan to meet*
> *Maggie and they were both going to Tokyo*
> *where they had jobs waiting, teaching*
> *Thur 11th Nov 1971 - A letter… from Jan. She*
> *says that Mark finishes in Antarctica next*
> *February and is planning some climbing tour*
> *through South America on his way back home*
> *Sun 9th Jan 1972 - Phone call… to Trevor who*
> *was leaving for India sometime next month*
> *Wed 30th Aug 1972 - Rich and Angie came up*
> *and we had a good evening sitting around*
> *talking. They are off to the States in about three*
> *weeks' time*

I clearly delighted in the wanderings of my friends
and created a role for myself as their occasional
chronicler. Unsettled and made restless by their
accounts I certainly was at times, but my entries do
not display the tinges of envy and resentment that
might be expected in such circumstances. Instead, as
if in some cosy command and control centre, I
envisaged their weaving of some global matrix with
hints of their underlying personal stories
occasionally showing through the fabric

> *Fri 3rd Dec 1971 - Had a letter from Alan and*
> *Maggie this morning. They are teaching English*
> *conversation in Tokyo*
> *Fri 10th Mar 1972 - Had a letter from Alan*
> *Spencer. He seems to have left Maggie in Tokyo*
> *and to be working his way back … He has a job*
> *on a ship and has just had a two-week shore leave*
> *in Red China, in Shanghai, from where he has*
> *travelled to Peking*

*Tue 16th May 1972 - Yesterday we had a card
from Trev and Viv in Kathmandu. They had just
spent a fortnight walking from Pokhara to
Annapurna base camp and back. Plan to be back
in about four months*
*Sat 3rd Jun 1972 - A letter from Mark,
postmarked Colorado. He says that he's planning
to be home in November. By then he will have
been out of the country for three years*
*Tue 20th Mar 1973 - A letter from Rich and
Angie this morning …there's those two in Santa
Cruz on Monterey Bay. Still feeling like a home
base for all my displaced wandering friends,
although their numbers are decreasing*

Unlike the friends who bought the tickets and plunged into their journeys, I dithered at the edge of commitment

*Sun 2nd May 1971 - I've been feeling again
lately that after this next year… I'd like to go
abroad and do something different for a year*
*Sat 5th Jun 1971 - I feel that if I don't go off soon
… for a year I never will. With the prospect of
buying such things as furniture coming soon,
there is less chance of mobility*

It was as if moving out of furnished accommodation and having to buy a few pieces of junk shop furniture might be enough to dash such dreams. However, as 1971 deepened into winter and one month after our head teacher's death, my diary reflected a strong sense of contentment with my work

*Thurs 2nd Dec 1971 - Feeling so much how
enjoyable my lot is this year, job-wise*

Nonetheless, the desire to be grabbing one last big adventure before finally subscribing fully to career and family was still tugging strongly, at others as well as me

> *Sun 12th Dec 1971 - John and Kathy were frantically calculating how much it would cost to buy a large van between six of us and go to India for six months. We made it £200 per head. We phoned Handford and he said he was interested but his job would probably go if he went ... John H arrived about 9 but said that he would have to remain in his present field for the next 2 - 3 years. If we don't have the right people it would not be worthwhile but we couldn't do it on a smaller number*
>
> *Mon 30th Dec 1971 - We talked more about India with John S. We phoned up Chris, who likes the idea*

The scheme was picking up steam, as we pulled into 1972

> *Sat 1st Jan 1972 - Dwelt on India for some time. There are slight anxieties that Chris and Mick won't be able to raise the cash in time. But these are not necessarily very realistic fears. Whatever happens, I should be writing a lot of these pages in distant lands*

The writing was on the wall and in my pages but the fantasy continued to fuel an optimism for the unfolding year. A series of near identical entries beat out the rhythm of this aspiration keeping it firmly on track

> *Tues 4th Jan 1972 - Chatted about the possibilities of some kind of sponsorship for our trip to India.... The main worry at the moment is that Chris and Mick will not get the money together, or at least start saving*

Keep facing forward, sunny side up

> *Sat 15th Jan 1972 - Chris and Mick both keen to*
> *come but they are worried that they will not be*
> *able to save the money in time*

The longest journey starts with the first building society deposit

> *Sun 16th Jan 1972 - Chris and Mick, I think, will*
> *get the money, and Colin and Sue are now*
> *definitely coming as well*

Be careful what you save for

> *Sun 13th Feb 1972 - With the £500 we have at*
> *the moment and the 500 we hope to save before*
> *the end of September, we would have enough to*
> *settle comfortably in Dorset – and nothing seems*
> *more attractive and fulfilling at the moment … I*
> *suddenly feel as though I have been brought back*
> *to my senses … India is now being questioned*

Pulling one little thread

> *Tues 7th Mar 1972 - I had decided to break the*
> *news that we weren't going to India and when I*
> *said this Mick revealed that he was getting*
> *pretty serious with Christine and had decided*
> *against it. Chris apparently has saved nothing*

*

Time to stop spinning, time to set a fixed bearing and pursue it. My interview for a school in the village of Evershot in rural Dorset was a first decisive step. As I was warmed on the morning of my interview by nurturing Spring sunshine and my friend's three-piece suit, the future was bursting into life around me

> *Mon 22nd May 1972 - The school was a very*
> *pleasant building – an old village school hall*
> *with new rooms built into it …*

There were four of us candidates. The girl from the coach - sensible blue suit, lacy ruffle at her neck, thinking about doing the Open University. A tall thin young man, thick brown suit, weak chin, stumblingly and excruciatingly polite. Me, long-haired, supercilious and cocky. A second woman, brash, no nonsense, looked like she had known her way around a punishment book or two. All of us of a similar age.

The head barrelled his way around the building on a lightening tour for the four of us

> ... It was designed to be open plan but the head had found it unworkable and now kept the shutters closed ... The head's class were all seated in long rows copying from textbooks in absolute silence. He asked them who had enjoyed the open plan system. No hands up. Who enjoyed it now that they were being taught? All hands up. This really put me off and as I waited to be interviewed. I wondered what I would do if I were offered the job ...

If I were offered the post and then declined to accept, I would be liable for my own expenses. The train fare would make a significant dent in our monthly budget.

Who would like to be marooned forever, day in day out, with this pompous, little bigot? No hands up. Who could slip beneath the surface in this educational backwater with no hope of eventual rescue or resuscitation? All hands up.

More disconcerting was the easy banter between the head and the forward woman. Perhaps they had studied together on the same course in exerting dubious authority over small children, with self-importance and insensitivity as elective modules? They began to talk quite openly about the enjoyable time they had spent together the previous evening in the pub!

> *... The interview was a bit more heartening, the managers were quite a good bunch ...*

I am surprised that I recorded no further details about the interview itself as I am still now raising one particular incident whenever conversations take a particular drift. One of the panel of half a dozen was introduced as the local squire. Until that day, I suppose I had assumed that such characters were inventions from a certain genre of nineteenth century novel or from mechanical and predictable situation comedies. Had I been forced to recognise that the position was a real and tangible one, then I might have assumed that squires had become extinct around the time of, say, the evolution of the motor car. But here he was, not rotund with mutton chop whiskers, but a tall, lanky young man, no more than half a dozen years my senior, in an understated but large checked suit in country colours, a patterned handkerchief in his breast pocket.

I responded to each of the panels' questions in turn, fumbling on the practicalities of teaching reading but soaring on the place of creativity in classrooms, and then it was the squire's turn.

'And tell me, Mr Miller, do you have any political interests?'

Political interests? I was completely thrown. Surely he does not mean do I vote in a certain direction? Perhaps he is referring to national policy making, Education Select Committees and the like? Or, maybe, the local Amersham 'Stop the 11+' campaign instigated by concerned and increasingly vocal parents?

'I'm sorry. I'm not sure that I completely – that I understand what you are asking me'

'Well, let me put it like this. If you were to move here would you be looking to start up a local Evershot Fascist Party?'

'A local –? Start up a local –?'

I stumbled and then paused to collect my thoughts, to formulate the killer answer. But my thoughts had been despatched to some different destination.

'No - I wouldn't. I wouldn't be starting up a local Evershot Fascist Party'.

After the individual grillings, we four candidates sat in an intense but stifled spirit of camaraderie, awaiting the judgement. The door opened, the air thickened, a heavy silence forced itself upon the room. The head circled us at our little table, like a predator high in the sky selecting its prey.

'We have had a lot of discussion and I have to say the governors and I came to different decisions'.

Five more careful steps around our backs.

'On this occasion I have agreed to go with the choice of the governors …'

Three more steps.

'… and we are offering you the post,' he said, laying a hand theatrically on the shoulder of the other male candidate who was already flushed with embarrassment and struggling to utter any words of gratitude.

To his drinking companion of the previous evening, the head said

'I'm sorry about all this but, if you'll wait in my office when we've finished, I have a colleague in the next village who has a vacancy coming up next term and I'll have a word with him on the phone.'

He extended his hand to the young woman with the lacy ruffle.

'I am sure that if you wish to work in Dorset and you keep applying for vacancies, you will sooner or later be successful'.

His hand remained firmly by his side as he turned towards me.

'Goodbye, Mr Miller!'

> *... On the train back. I was sitting next to the girl who had been on the coach and she talked non-stop all the way to Bournemouth. Feeling depressed, I decided to have a meal on my expenses. Sat there in the old three-piece suit with the golden evening sun on the flashing green landscape, eating steak. Bottle of wine, fruit salad, coffee and cigars. Felt much better.*

Options narrowed, resolution rode in, and within hours the future was sealed

> *Thur 25th May 1972 - Having scuttled the idea of teaching in Dorset we thought about and decided on the West Riding of Yorkshire.*

*

Len Marsh, the organiser of my teacher training course, remained an influential figure and the main person to whom I turned for careers advice. Although his manoeuvring to introduce ex-students and head teachers to each other would become unacceptable under subsequent employment law and practices, at the time it seemed a worthy attempt to spread and reinforce the educational approach for which he was such a persuasive advocate.

While passing through the phase of wishing to travel and work abroad, I had rejected his judgement

> *Mon 15th Nov 1971 - I have written to VSO*
> [Voluntary Services Overseas] *tonight feeling*

that this is the best course of action (again). I was temporarily thrown by Len Marsh and was getting these delusions of ending up as some gasbag on education somewhere. It is very attractive but I don't really feel it is me to have a fixed idea of what I want to be doing at 40 and concentrate all my attention on that

But after making the decision to try for a post in the West Riding of Yorkshire, I contacted him again

Thurs 25th May 1972 - Plucked up courage (why it was needed I don't know) and phoned Len Marsh to see what he knew. He immediately warmed to the idea and started making mental notes of people to phone. He's such a nice helpful person. He thinks that we shall probably have to stay here until January

Fri 9th Jun 1972 - A letter from Len Marsh was waiting for me at school today. He had been in touch with Ted Tattersall from Rossington [near Doncaster] who was 'very anxious' to meet me. It seems as though Len has really been working for me

Thurs 14th Sept 1972 - Had a letter from Ted Tattersall this morning, offering me a definite job for next summer or maybe Easter

I had obtained a new post – it was a time in which teaching vacancies were plentiful – without my new boss-to-be even having met me. And, similarly, I had accepted without even viewing the place. Perhaps, such occurrences might be a progressive counter balance to the machinations of squires and rural bombasts down in the county of my birth? Certainly, for me at the time, not having been hardened by much of a track record in failed interviews (just failed exams), being seen as a desirable appointee must have renewed my self-confidence after the miserable rejection at Evershot.

At the next half term holiday, I readily took the opportunity to see what I had committed myself to

>Weds 1st Nov 1972 - We decided to drive out to have a look at Rossington and its environs.... I had had visions of little colliery villages dominated by huge pithead wheels, but there wasn't much sign of this at all, and some of the places we passed through we were favourably impressed with. Rossington was probably the least pleasant of the lot
>
>Thurs 2nd Nov 1972 - Drove over to meet Ted Tattersall and to have a look around the school ... I began to feel (it to be) a very exciting and rich place. He kept on about how hard they all worked and I remembered my psychology [degree by private study] and worried a little. But then I remembered Morris saying identical things ... and me never thinking I was working hard, well, hard, but pleasantly and not under a lot of strain ... When I asked if he wanted to grill me further he said that he had phoned Len Marsh last night and was satisfied
>
>Sun 11th Feb 1973 - In the afternoon we drove over to Rossington and I was formally offered the job

In a topsy-turvy turnaround, the most formal part of my interview came last of all. In the head teacher's study, I sat with him and the school's chair of governors and her dog, all of us humans in armchairs. I have no memory of our actual conversation and neither does my diary carry a record, but I do remember the coal fire in the grate and being aware that the source of this solid heat would have been hacked from beneath ground no distance from where we were sitting. The fat and flatulent chocolate and white spaniel stirred and grunted occasionally at our feet, one or the other of my conversational partners leaned forwards to give the fire a proprietorial poke and the grey afternoon light faded outside the window and from all across the huge estate of Coal Board houses

> *... Ted Tattersall said that he was looking for someone who had a big heart, which he thought I had, and a bit of scholarship as well made it even better. In the face of such a compliment, I couldn't refuse the job*

Two hundred and fifty miles or so from my Dorset debacle – but cultural galaxies distant – (and in the face of such flattery) I sensed an ideological home. With its own deep seam of traditional loyalties and observances, the West Riding represented a conservatism I could respect. Far more so than the radicalism that I might once have pinned my hopes upon

> *Sat 8th Jul 1972 - Went down to Deptford, where there was a gathering called Alternatives in Education or something. It was a sort of Alternative Education's pop festival. Great to see this happening, but I felt the discussion groups weren't biting deeply enough into issues. Rather condescending attitude towards anyone inside the system. Liverpool Free School were there with John Ord. Saw the little girl who sang 'Brand-New Pair of Roller Skates' on the recent TV programme about the school*

The close camaraderie of mining communities, people's seemingly dour but dry-humoured matter-of-factness and a more firmly grounded set of values

– these were all images that I had accrued during my cultural meanderings. The reality, at least during the first months of our geographical and social upheaval, proved very far from these romanticised musings.

First, there was my unanticipated reaction to leaving a place for which I had thought I felt little affection

> *Sat 14th Apr 1973 - At last, I have felt something about moving. Waves of sadness today have almost brought me to tears. For all the faults of the place itself, at least Amersham was a small enough place, compared to London, to get a vague feeling of community*

Then there was our financial position.

> *Sat 6th Jan 1973 - We have spent a week vainly searching for a house. Although there are house prices within our capabilities (£6,000) and this is quite reassuring in a time of soaring prices, nevertheless we have not been able to secure anything ... Our position at the moment is that we ... stretch our deposit and repayments to the limit on a nasty modern semi*
>
> *Sun 5th Mar 1973 - Conversation has got back time and time again to how badly off we are going to be next year. I estimate that my take home pay is going to be about £23 per week and the mortgage repayments will be £11. There will be an incredibly thin margin between the possible and the impossible. It seems as though we will recover in three or four years' time but how long a period of desperation does it take to stamp home for life a bitter and cynical attitude?*

Despite the conservative streak to my character that had encouraged me to save, budget and not over-reach, almost as soon as we signed our first mortgage deal, oil prices trebled, inflation careered ferociously around every supermarket aisle and mortgage rates were yanked from our grip. The time for diary entries was rapidly reducing because of my strict schedule of spare time study, the demands of my new job and the birth of our first son.

But finances do appear as a frequent and frightening preoccupation during my increasingly more irregular entries

Sun 7th Oct 1973 - I'm not very committed to much at the moment, except keeping my neck above water in an atmosphere of rising prices and mortgage rates and armed only with a well below national average take-home pay

Long before a knowledge of alternative protein sources, our weekly budget allowed us a tightly-managed and unvarying allowance of one half pound of mince and the same of liver between us. Our house fell immediately into negative equity and rate increases further exacerbated our loss of control. The bank manager requested that I talk him through our monthly spending and, biting back feelings of abandonment by the guardians of civic and financial probity that I had secretly sought to appease for so long, I spread my hopeless calculations before him. We circled possibilities that crashed each to earth with every futile reckoning until, in sticky desperation, he curtailed our collaboration.

'Well, you just have to make more economies. That's all there is to it!'

Too raw, any of this, for my diary. Best buried at the time lest it consolidated despair, squeezed tight on any breath of optimism. Still almost too painful, even now, to justify its airing in painted prose.

And then, the new job

> *Weds 2nd May 1973 - Last night I was seriously doubting that I would settle ... I also don't feel I have a loud enough voice for this school, it is something I have not perfected on purpose. The kids were playing up a bit this afternoon and I had my first feeling, ever, that I might not be able to cope. Will not get dispirited*
> *Sun 6th May 1973 - I have had one week at school and have found it quite challenging. I feel that I will get on top of the situation fairly easily. The kids were definitely trying me out at first, but towards the end of the week I could see a lot of signs, just facial expressions or a request carried out without an expression of resentment, which told me I was winning. Thinking on it, it is probably good diary material to comment on foggy, segmented, first impressions of the new job*

'Will not get dispirited ...' 'Will get on top of the situation fairly easily ...' It is soothing self-talk, of a sort that is easily parodied, and not a style that I can generally detect in my diaries. Was my diary, during these tumultuous months, attesting to a buried optimism? Or was it a creation, self-deception, a voice from nowhere attempting to talk me into a concocted hope?

One incident more than any other from this period has remained vividly alive, not mentioned in my diary but gouged deeply into memory nonetheless. For Christmas 1973, we planned a simple day at home with our son. My wife shopped with scrupulous attention to our finances deliberately saving just one 5p coin in her purse, our very last money, for one holiday extravagance – a copy of the

Radio Times so that we could indulge ourselves, exercise some control, over our television viewing. The shopkeeper placed the magazine on the counter. She gave him the 5p.

'It's 10p,' he said.

She reminded him that it cost 5p.

'Not this issue,' he replied.

It was a double issue, Christmas and New Year combined. Hence the 10p.

She had to hand it back to him, struggle to find words.

And leave the shop empty-handed.

*

After full day-to-day pages from my first two years as a teacher, the empty and unrecorded months and terms from 1973 spoke, rather than recorded, volumes. And in that absence, was the struggle to overcome financial despair and self-pity, to prevent these from finding angry expression in response to the kindly concern of old friends. Later, towards the end of 1974 and with a second baby born, the topic that threatened to rip the present from a grounding past was sleep. How could culture, politics or psychology capture my conversational engagement when set against the anarchy of broken nights, the lack of rest and replenishment?

But, after the dismay, these pages do also outline the recovering of morale. Firstly, a new friend made because my Austin A40 van had broken down

Sun 30th Jun 1973 - I asked Hillary if she would give me a lift in on Friday. We got chatting and, besides being a very likeable person, I found that she had experienced the same difficulties in

settling in. She thought that Ted tends to over-romanticise the social nature of the staff when he speaks elsewhere about school

Then I was given a class of my own, rather than the make-shift sharing arrangement of my first term

Sun 30th Sep 1973 - Exactly a fortnight ago I intended to make a diary entry about how apprehensive and depressed I felt about going back to school. One day back though was enough to convince me that I could have a great year with these kids. They have an incredibly positive attitude towards work and never complain. They also get on with each other extremely well and create an atmosphere of affection. Much more about this, no doubt, later

Well, in the event, not much more really. Very little by way of written account but, nevertheless, memories that have remained clear and strong. The nine-year old boy who was at school by eight each morning, often before me, building up his painting of a buzzard feather by patient feather over a period of weeks. The atmosphere of quiet industry that greeted me most mornings when I arrived to find my self-organising early attenders settled to various tasks. The mother who, unbeknown to me, had visited the head to complain that her son's schooling did not sound at all like the proper education that she had received, had then been persuaded by him into being my classroom helper for a morning a week and was then introduced to me as a willing volunteer with no mention being made of the complaint. (She eventually became an enthusiast for the school's methods.)

Teaching myself about musical notation before passing this on, keeping one step ahead of my guitar and recorder groups, wind instruments for our poorest children stored in a school collection and dipped regularly in disinfectant. Every pupil in the school playing music at some level with scores written for all by an extremely talented staff member. Borrowing my wife's old dissection kit, buying a dead pigeon from Doncaster market one lunchtime on a visit with my van filled with kids, learning about the techniques biologists employed for pinning back at each stage, detailed labelled sketches and additional library research into the arrangement and function of organs to bolster their written accounts and self-produced textbooks. Tricky negotiations with the school cook to store our increasingly dismembered pigeon in one of her fridges. A father asking me, somewhat surreptitiously, whether I could use a dead fox! All gloriously unfettered or hideously unacceptable – it really does depend on one's fundamental priorities – by today's standards.

The whole class down at a local drainage ditch measuring current speeds and plumbing the depths - the height of busy educational involvement. Generating questions we none of us could answer – did water at the surface flow at the same speed as water at the bottom, and at the sides in comparison to the centre? Devising measuring instruments and investigative strategies. Returning to the field, pooling our observations, debating conclusions against the evidence, and developing methods of charting and graphing to communicate our findings.

It was in the middle of a particularly busy and relatively noisy morning that Ted brought in Sir Alec Clegg, the inspirational Chief Education Officer who, more than any other individual, had passionately pioneered and created a Local Education Authority in which the virtues of a 'progressive' approach could flourish. Almost pushing him to one side, my children continued with their recording of visitors to our bird table, their behaviour and flight patterns. While I struggled to suppress a sense of deference, present an articulate account of what we trying to achieve and keep a lid on the most exuberant in my charge, he nodded quietly but otherwise gave little by way of reaction. I awaited some sort of judgement apprehensively and was both surprised and delighted when Ted informed me later that Clegg had given his approval.

The educational idealism embedded in the old West Riding was forged in hardship though and I was reminded of this graphically during the 1974 Miners' Strike and the 'Three Day Week'

> *Sat 16th Feb 1974 - Yesterday Hilary found a girl crying in her class and discovered that she hadn't eaten for nearly 2 days!*

This little girl's father had, for whatever reason, not received strike pay. A colleague arranged for a box of groceries to be left anonymously that evening, under the cover of darkness, on the family's doorstep.

*

With the passing of my degree in 1974, and a consequent small salary increase, my barely contained sense of terror from previous months began to ease

> *Sat 22nd Jun 1974 - I shall soon be out of the desperation – we were not able to afford enough food for ourselves through the winter – but only really into an acceptable degree of poverty. I'm fairly happy with that but I am smarting after*

> *the last year's experiences and worried about the*
> *future ... too self-involved, unrefreshed, I have*
> *so much less to give*

From a distance of more than forty years, I can see my idealism towards my job as more complex than I perhaps recognised at the time. The two schools I worked in remain as creative, thoughtful and energetic enterprises in my mind. I would have loved to attend either as a child myself and I would have wished them for my own sons. But, this vocational commitment came at a price. It would have been possible to apply for promotions elsewhere, to pursue an extra increment for additional responsibilities and thus begin to relieve us of our financial worries.

Instead, I remember the distaste, contempt almost, that I felt for one or two colleague determined to advance their careers through any avenue. I presented myself in my diary sometimes as loyal to a particular philosophy, as a 'believer' - and I was. However, with hindsight, I now also recognise an element of fear that I would be unable to command the authority I assumed to be necessary for a 'management position'.

*

After a year or so of life in our small semi-detached house on a characterless, open-plan, new estate we were reminded of the bigger vistas that had occupied imaginations in earlier days

> *Sun 30th Jun 1974 - Handford, Sue and a guy*
> *called John called in last night – on their way to*
> *the Himalaya. They are having the first few days*
> *to sort out teething troubles – two punctures*
> *yesterday. Planning to be there in three weeks,*
> *covering 350 miles a day...*

I used my diary to make light of the contrast between our current life and the adventures of our old friend

> ... They must have had that lovely feeling that, after all the doubts and the panic, there is the cathartic feeling of freedom, the joy of a lot of travelling to do, the luxury of uncomfortable nights' sleep, and the excitement of long, boring endless roads. Saying – 'Goodbye, take care, look after yourselves' – as these three crammed into their cramped Land Rover in Cranswick Way [our address], one of the places from which all true adventures should proceed

And so they left, casting off connections and predictability with each new border crossed. No word was expected and none came until we received an unexpected phone call many weeks later

> Tues 20th Aug 1974 - While we were at Swindon [at my parents' house] we had a 'Guess who this is?' phone call. It was Handford calling from Mount Vernon Hospital in Northwood. They (had been) travelling through Iran and had to swerve out to avoid a boy on a bike and in doing so hit a big lorry. Sue and John didn't fare too badly but Handford was scraped along the ground by the locked back wheels of the lorry. They were the double set variety and if the driver had once taken his foot off the clutch Andy would almost certainly have been killed. He said that one foot was unrecognisable as a foot as was an arm and that his right hip was dislocated. It seems that the accident was only the beginning of his problems. He was taken to a small local hospital where the sanitary conditions were so bad that he immediately caught a fever which ran

at 103 for a couple of days. There were no
nursing facilities and Andy had to supervise his
own medical care, fighting off being given
morphia for constipation. One arm was in
plaster while the other was on a drip. Bowls of
food would be brought him and, unless a visitor
came over and fed him, it would be taken away
again after a while. In the end, Vincent [his
brother] *flew out to Tehran hospital and*
brought Andy back from there.

*

As a last blast of 1960s experimentation, as a challenge to the prospect of a lifestyle without challenge and innovation, we agreed to buy an old house in north Lincolnshire on a joint mortgage with my colleague, Hilary. House renovation was a particular interest among a number of the teachers with whom we worked, spurred on by one person who was an architect turned primary school teacher. In this inexpensive area of the country we could take ownership of a crumbling detached house with a third of an acre of orchard and vegetable patches.

My diary reveals a dreamy optimism about the prospect of communal living and attempting to become more self-sufficient away from a life of urban anonymity

Christmas Eve 1974 - We are settling into The
Laurels and digging a burrow deep enough, it
seems, to huddle in for a good many years

Another aspect of my deeper career aspirations at that time, visible to me now between the lines I wrote, was my seeking out of inspirational bosses. My first head had died after I had been only one year in his employ and Ted Tattersall left after a similar interval, promoted to a senior, and influential, role in the Local Education Authority. His replacement was a cynical and burnt-out character drafted in, it seemed, from a school in a more affluent area where he had been the subject of various parental complaints. He openly mocked us, his new staff, for working an extra hour or two each evening and delighted in revving his car engine in the yard, counting down the minutes before the 'home time' bell when he could roar away.

It was time for me to step away from following leaders, however committed, and make my own way

> *Christmas Eve 1974 - I applied for, and have been accepted for a post as a trainee educational psychologist in Doncaster*

Within a year or two I had lost contact with my former colleagues, only to reunite briefly with them decades later

> *Mon 16th Nov 2009 - To Ted Tattersall's funeral ... I was five minutes late and squeezed into the packed church standing with the men of the British Legion, the sea scouts just along the way. The vicar, pure Yorkshire, had known Ted a while and talked of his early years, including war years in the Far East and a few escapades ... His granddaughter spoke finally about 'Grandpa', straight and true, and it was very moving. He was very much loved and a popular local character*

There was also a wonderful anecdote that pulled me and the whole congregation back to much earlier times. The clergyman said he had visited Ted in hospital only days before his death and he was fulminating at articles in the national newspapers – 'Just look what they're trying to do now. We've got to stop them.' No need to mention who or what, we all got the drift, felt the need once again to fight the righteous fight.

In the same vein, of the same blood and matter, my mentor and guide from my teaching days was also at the funeral, his sparkling enthusiasm dimmed with age by only by a minute degree

> ... Len Marsh, still looking young, curious and impish, although he must be well into his 70s. As I squeezed his arm at one point though, there was a lot of suit jacket to grip before I came to bone ... was (I) ever in London, knew a club, terrible people really but one of the few places in central London where one could eat and hear each other's conversation. A moving celebratory day in many ways – and lots of twinkly photos of Ted all around the room

The trickle of entries diminished even further through 1974. My diaries were opened less and less frequently. Apart from a limp attempt at a few pages in 1977, it was to be seven years before circumstances provoked me into completing a brand new volume.

In the mid-1970s I had a sense, an inaccurate one it transpired, that my life had settled into a secure and predictable pattern with loose ends tied and tidied

> Christmas Eve 1974 - A whole term in which I've written nothing ... Handford came up a few weeks ago with his American physiotherapist, Lyn, and today we had a card announcing that they were getting married. Luke was born on November 27
> Wed 19th Nov 1975 - I am now 29, with two children and a "good" job

III

10. GATHERED FROM COINCIDENCE

Purposes can evolve and change. What precipitated me into writing a diary in the first place need not be the reason to persist.

A key event for me in this and many other respects was a fall in the Alps in 1992 whilst retreating from an unsuccessful attempt on the Grand Combin in Switzerland

> *Mon 3rd Aug 1992 - We finally got back to the snow at about 7 with thunder cracking and a mist closing down the visibility. Within one or two steps of stepping down the soft snow my feet shot away from under me and I was moving very fast and unable to get it back under control. How to say it without clichés? I thought I was going to die. The slope was steep and went on for about 2,000 feet, there was little to stop a fall. I was aware of the fact that I hadn't become detached from my axe, I was talking to myself coherently and fast, trusting on the rock break to arrest my fall, hitting it and keeping moving, fighting against accepting this was it.*
>
> *I hit the 3rd rock break and stopped. I crouched by the axe, shaking but surprisingly clear-headed, telling myself to do nothing despite the dark, being miles from the hut, the thunder and now the lightning. When the shaking stopped I tried to cross the snow to the next band of rock and shale and then across to the next. In the dark I eventually heard Peter shouting (he had had two slides as well) and we proceeded down shale and snow.*

> *Lower down with the mist lifted, there was a rock fall above me and three big rocks, one the size of a dustbin, came cascading down. I fought with reduced reserves against a sense of the inevitable and the biggest one trundled by only 15 feet away. Exhausted at the hut at least 16 hours after leaving it. The warden was very kind and cooked us something special after most people had gone to bed. Fearing delayed shock invading my sleep I turned in*

My Alpine climbing career had always been rather lacklustre and surviving this fall removed all further ambition in these directions. Soon afterwards and back in Derbyshire, a much less sensational slip was enough for me to decide that my rock climbing days too were probably over.

These events prompted me to take seriously at last the business of making a will and my diaries made an unexpected appearance at my meeting with the solicitor I consulted.

> *Mon 16th Nov 1992 - First question re the will – burial or cremation? Pass. I then said that the romantic in me fancied rotting in the ground but the pragmatist approved when others went for cremation. The most emotional event for me was the destination of these diaries. I supposed that they might get thrown away and that my boys might then want to look at them later in their lives. Or that friends might want to dip into them. And what about the embarrassment to the 'curator' if people found me more critical than they had expected?*

As I was musing aloud about the likelihood of anybody having an interest after my departure, the solicitor said with some tenderness that if her own father had written a diary she would very much wish to read it. Devising a formula for the disposal of my slender and straightforward estate was quickly achieved and, as my parents had retained no sentimental artefacts from their pasts, there was nothing to pass on. We spent the major part of our meeting therefore ruminating on the future of my diaries. Eventually, and between us, we worded the relatively lengthy stipulation that my three sons should decide between them on the diaries' future, only destroying them if and when all three were in agreement to do so.

*

Future generations again entered my considerations after a weekend visit to friends

> *Sat 26th Jan 2002 - (N Yorks) We sat eating and drinking until 3am, talking particularly about my grandmother Beatrice and Jonathan's grandfather whose brief and illicit First World War diary from the front, he has recently acquired*

Although I wrote no more about it, that slim little book with its battered red cover and neatly written entries describing transportation to France, jovial accounts of football matches in the lull before action and then a silence, made a deep impression. Never mind the content for a minute. Just to hold it, make physical contact with my fingers where its author had first placed his, was a moving experience. And maybe it influenced this entry made a couple of weeks later

> *Tue 5th Feb 2002 - Thirty-five years after beginning all this writing and scribbling I think I am now clear who I am writing for. At first, and still at times, it is about picking and storing*

from my experiences for my own satisfaction.
And about making sense. But ultimately, I now
think these diaries are for my grandchildren. You
don't exist yet but I hope to meet you someday

Another fifteen years on and my second wife and I have seven grandchildren between us.

And what was written there in relative maturity now feels forced and twee.

A firm sense of my intended audience still eludes me.

*

My early literary gurus had soon let me down. Kerouac died young, sozzled through and through. Not on the road but in his mother's house, to which he had retreated some time earlier. Salinger lived as a recluse for decades with rumours suggesting a complex and unsettled man. Although I haven't yet re-read those books that shaped my sense of purpose as a youngster, I still retain a respect for them. Just not for their authors as guides to how I might live my life.

Bob Dylan, another early influence, once said that fame is a curse and nostalgia is death. Cheerful old sod. I can't vouch for the fame bit from personal experience but I've tried not to bury my head in bygone days and so miss the onward-rushing present.

Hence, before this current project, I had limited my ruminations on the past and felt only the occasional impulse to pull a year from the shelf and rifle idly through. I've used them once or twice though when talking with old friends about times spent together years before. 'Was so-and-so there that night with us in the pub?' or, 'Was that before X was going out with

Y or after they'd split up?' Their pleasure at having such queries nailed has delighted me, bolstering the flimsy rationale for my jottings. And usually, while we are setting one particular record straight, I will be asked further questions about other incidents on the off-chance there may also be stray details in those areas to shore up time's erosion.

I have been carrying thin slivers from the collective memories of many others.

*

A new motivation for persisting with my diary writing also arises now that my record spans a wide period of my life. The making of unexpected links across large stretches of time, the establishing of unexpected coincidences.

Again, from that weekend visit to friends in North Yorkshire

> Sun 27th Jan 2002 - Another late, slow breakfast, with lots of talking … and then a drive out to Ravenscar on the coast … We picked our way down beneath cliffs to the desolate shore, through a landscape that attracted the biologist in Jonathan … Driving back at teatime Jonathan, upon hearing my educational history, said I must have been at Goldsmiths at the same time as Kaye S. When I said that we had gone to a party of hers, they said they had been to one too. Jonathan looked up the date in his diary – Nov '68 – and then back home I looked in mine – 16/11/68. We had all been there!!

I had originally met Tink and Jonathan in 1988 when she was a mature student with me and Jonathan a lecturer in the neighbouring Biology Department. I was then getting to know them better some fourteen years after that.

Sun 17th Nov 1968 - Last night Kathy and I
went up to Kaye S's place in Kensington for her
21st. The attic flat is a superb place – we were
both green. Andy (Handford) seemed to be very
happy chattering away with Kaye's sister,
Loveday. We were lucky to get a lift at about 2
back to Forest Hill.

Discovering that we had once been together in the same room in London twenty years before the time we thought we had first met, and thirty-four years before this discovery dawned on us, gave me a frisson of excitement, like a child at a magic show first unsettled by a sense of the uncanny undermining the assumed predictability of the material world.

*

The making of links retrospectively has lately begun to serve a more profound purpose than merely the establishment of coincidences, highly rewarding and pleasurable though these still are

Sat 9th Sept 1967 - A quick meal after work ...
before zooming off to Bridport on my bike to see
Roger and Val. They have a fantastic house ...
We laid some linoleum in the kitchen and finally
got to bed about 1. I slept in a fantastic attic
room which contained absolutely no furniture
except my bed and an ashtray

My old school friend Roger and his wife Val were the first of my acquaintances to buy a house and, although I had a vaguely formed notion that 'mortgages' somehow automatically and irrevocably extinguished the life force, I was also reassured by their anchoring domesticity

Wed 20th Sept 1967 - After dinner I drove out to
Abbotsbury and then on to Bridport to visit

*Roger and Val. Also present were Steve and
Martin and Ivan showed up later. The latter has
bought a new scooter and wishes to talk of
nothing else. When the others began to get fed up
with talking about this subject, Ivan stormed out
in a dramatic exit. I left Bridport at about 11.30
and came home via Dorchester. The journey was
a cold and lonely one. The cool full moon gave an
ephemeral glow to the Wessex countryside*

Within a week, I was back in Bridport prior to
departing for London and my second year at
Goldsmiths College

*Wed 27th Sept 1967 - After dinner I drove out to
Bridport to say goodbye to Roger and Val ... We
spent the whole evening just talking ...Roger
gave me a small spool of tape which he suggested
exchanging instead of letters. I left at about 11
and decided to come home along the coast road.
Between Swyre and Abbotsbury I ran into a
thick layer of sea mist and had to drive along
that deserted road in low gear in order to
generate enough light to see the white line by*

In retrospect, the brief descriptions of riding my
Lambretta from Bridport to Weymouth late at night
have fulfilled the purpose of capturing a mood and
moment. I would not have recalled these incidents
had I not written about them, and the remembered
sensations that they trigger are richly comforting
and, despite the cold and fog, very warming.

However, although I originally romanticised the
sense of connection between my friends and myself
there were developments in the future that I had
been unable to envisage

(email, late Nov 2009):

'Hi Ivan

... I do want to thank you for encouraging me as a youngster. I knew as a kid I was interested in books, the outdoors, the life of the mind and the heart, but didn't find a lot of role models on Westham estate to help in knowing how to realise these ambitions. You took an interest in us youngsters in the Field Club and I do remember walking home from Newton's Cove one summer evening in intense conversation when I must have been around 15 or 16 - the topic of the conversation is long gone to me now. The comic absurdity of some of your performances - Field Club talks, my 1969 wedding, evenings at Roger and Val's - stay with me and I treasure laughing out loud with, cliches though they may be, aching sides and tears in the eyes.

You have often provided a good balance for me between encouraging my writing and pronouncements whilst also puncturing my forays into pretentiousness. I've valued all that, Ivan.

I really hope the medication works for you and I am thinking of you. It is a beautiful autumn day out my window here at the university and I must return to hitting some targets. Or somebody. I'll be in touch again soon and hope to be able to get down your way to see you before too long'.

*

Fri 10th Sept 2010 - Changed into my funeral gear in a Little Chef car park just west of Dorchester ... In the church I was so pleased to see Roger and Val sitting there, I had been looking at their Facebook photos from Australia only days earlier. They arrived back at 7.30 this morning. The funeral was fairly formal C of E at Ivan's request, the wicker casket at the front. My tears started as soon as I sat down and came frequently during the whole service. Roger did one of the eulogies which I was pleased about ... He [Ivan] married Pat three weeks ago, although very ill, so that she would get his pension - ever the union man. Marilyn and Noreen [Ivan's sisters] were both splendid – noisy, emotional, just this side of tarty. Reception at the West Bay Hotel, a walk over the shingle to look at the breakers, violent ... as ever, in a stormy haze. 'This boy,' said Noreen, squeezing my shoulder repeatedly, 'this boy has come all the way from the Westham Estate'. Ivan had apparently once entered a crowded room with M and N and said 'My name is Cinderella; do you know my sisters?'
Indeed.

I have a deep sense of loss at the moment

Having a record from which to sample the trajectory of friendships over the course of a whole lifetime has proved extremely satisfying and a totally unforeseen outcome. I know that when I set out in 1967 I would have been incapable of imagining a future so far ahead (way beyond Orwell's 1984 barrier) in which some of us who had been young together would actually cease to be.

And despite all the changes that fifty years have brought, my friends Roger and Val continue to live in the house where we laid the kitchen linoleum when they first moved in

> *Sun 2nd Oct 2011 - (Bridport) A lovely evening with Roger and Val and his Mum, Simone. She is 90 soon, articulate, with a point of view and good left wing politics. The conversation seems far more precious now, now that Ivan's death has reminded me that the time scale for all this is finite*

Acknowledgements

My thanks are due to my colleagues at Nottingham Writers Studio – Frances Thimann, Angela Barton, Gaynor Backhouse and Paul Anderson – for their critical insights throughout the development of this book. I am also very grateful to Rob Tresidder for his assiduous proof reading and to Vally Miller for the cover photograph and design and her unflagging support and encouragement. They have all helped to make this a better book than it would otherwise have been but all remaining weaknesses, of course, remain mine alone.

HANGING IN THE BALANCE

Andy Christopher Miller

A collection of writing about survival in
relationships and climbing

*'Who can say when or how hope springs? Today like
a ray of sunlight, a small book has landed on my desk
... It may already be a collector's item ... For there is a
breath of humanity in this book ... Having this book
in my hands for half an hour was like sitting on the
grass with my back against a tree. It made me
sway...'*
Ed Drummond - Poet, activist and leading
British rock climber. In *Mountain*

*'This brave, fragile pamphlet of four essays and six
poems deftly tells the story of hanging in the balance
as climber, father, companion, husband, club-member
and divorcee. It begins with a crag rescue and ends
with the challenge of Christmas Day alone, 'without
self-pity or cynicism.' This is the best writing I've read
for ages. Better than whole books of empty narrative,
this little bit of autobiography climbs through the
important things in life. It will repay re-reading'.*
Professor Terry Gifford - Director of the
International Festival of Mountaineering
Literature. In *High*

Amcott Press   Published 1988

WHILE GIANTS SLEEP

Andy Christopher Miller

Andy Miller's prose and poetry has won a range of awards and commendations. Daisy Goodwin, the judge for the 2011 international Yeovil Literary Prize, described him as having '. . . *a distinctive voice. . .*' and his prize-winning poem 'Attempting to Interfere' as being '. . . *mysterious but repaying a close reading*'. His long out-of-print booklet 'Hanging in the Balance' also attracted critical acclaim and is reprinted here in full. This new anthology displays a twin focus on mountaineering, rock climbing and outdoor adventure and on relationships across the adult life span.

'This collection pulses with life and energy …
Previously published and unpublished work spanning forty-two years is combined in this book, providing an intimate overview of a life lived on the edge in the most literal sense … Miller's writing is sometimes humorous, deeply personal, and full of richly detailed observations, part of a continually developing tradition of walking and climbing literature'.

Aly Stoneman, *Left Lion*, Nottingham

Amcott Press   2nd Edition 2015

THE NAPLES OF ENGLAND

Andy Christopher Miller

The War is over and a generation returns home to build peace, determined to create a new society, protected from cradle to grave. This memoir of family, truth and secrets tells of the author's growing up in seaside Britain in the 1950s and early 1960s.

'... *a wonderful book by a writer who deserves wide recognition ... anyone yet to read it has a real treat in store'*
John Lindley, Cheshire Poet Laureate & Manchester Cathedral Poet

'... *much more than regional nostalgia. The writing can shift from lovingly recalled detail to moments of powerful experience'*
Tony Jones, Winner 2016 Writers Guild of Great Britain, Best Radio Play

'... *touches upon some universal themes ... as relevant to a child of the grimy north as to one brought up in coastal Dorset ... lyrical, subtle, original and surprising'*
Chris Thompson, Radio & Television Writer ('The Archers, Heartbeat, Emmerdale, stand-alone Radio 4 plays)

'... *funny, moving and perceptive by turns ... this vivid and touching account of a time of hope and innocence has darker currents, hinted at many times throughout'*
Frances Thimann, Author, - *November Wedding'*

'... *a moving, funny and compelling account of growing up in small-town Britain ... sheer warmth, honesty and fine detail'*
Megan Taylor, Author - *'The Lives Of Ghosts'*

Amcott Press   Published 2015